"Concerned about where your (whether you're a leader of a for-profit or non-profit enterprise, you should read this book. Organizational strength comes through the relationship with its stakeholders. Robert Nitschke provides a fresh perspective on the importance of collaboration to the future of any enterprise, and shines a bright light on the definitions and suggested tactics that will help move any organization to a more sustainable growth path."
Patrick Snow,
International Best-Selling Author of *Creating Your Own Destiny*

"The insights Robert shares about how to take collaboration to an entirely new level – inside and outside the organization – makes this a must read. Being able to use this powerful new approach to directly impact your customer and incorporate social media is critical to the future survival of every organization."
Blaine Millet, CEO, WOM10 Inc., Co-Author *Creating and Delivering Totally Awesome Customer Experiences*

"Robert's book is essential reading for any leader interested in the growth of a sustainable business. If you read only one book on what collaboration means to a company, make it this one!"
Matt Sauri, CEO, Wimmer Solutions, Inc.

"Business visioneers are posing the thought that we are in a window of time where businesses as we know and understand them, must transform to a more effective state of organization and execution of what they do in their markets. These dramatic transition periods have happened before. Robert has painted the vision of just such a picture, the Collaborative Enterprise. He has captured the business principles and characteristics in words, exceedingly well. *Creating a Collaborative Enterprise* defines a standard for business leaders to work toward using strategic planning and constant improvement techniques. I compliment the author for addressing the entire enterprise in his work. It allows the reader to think about the value of these insights, enterprise-wide. The author also presents advice on the keys to effective change in a business environment, the organizational culture and the process of evolving. Thank you Robert for defining a standard, *The Collaborative Enterprise*."
Michael J. Franz, Certified Business Advisor, Washington Small Business Development Center

"Business books are a 'dime a dozen'. *Creating a Collaborative Enterprise: Retool Your Organization to Dominate Your Markets* is worth its weight in gold. Using clear and concise language, Robert Nitschke offers up an extremely provocative template for an innovative and successful business model. His emphasis on the *all the major stakeholders* and his focus on creating an 'open society' within an organization should be textbook reading for all leaders. Ignore this book at your peril... it could make all the difference to your business and to your career."
Ed Gardner, President: The Journey: Legacy and Leadership Coaching; An Executive Coaching Firm

"I see the strategies, tactics and suggested execution methods within this book as an excellent roadmap for any leader to follow if they need to increase their companies position within their industry, no matter where they are located in the US or around the world; this book should be in every potential or established leaders library"
Charles Manger, CEO, Clean Power Holdings, Inc.

"*Creating a Collaborative Enterprise* reflects Robert Nitschke's understanding of the difference between conceptual thinking and tactical action. He has done a great job at explaining what an organization can gain from being a collaborative company and then also provides very usable suggestions for an action plan. Well done!"
Dominic Dobson
Chief Development Officer, LeMay - America's Car Museum, Indy 500 Fastest Rookie in History, 1988

Robert Nitschke captures how businesses need to evolve to enable them to succeed and thrive in the future business climate in his book *Creating a Collaborative Enterprise-Retool your organization to dominate your market.*
Paul Bowman, CEO, Great Lakes ComNet

"Robert focuses the subject of collaboration on the entire corporation and its ecosystem in a way that is meaningful and easily understood with this book - it offers an excellent blueprint to create a great environment that breeds success and longevity".
Michael Pisterzi, CEO Adaptix Corporation

"Robert Nitschke has created an excellent description of how best to approach any needed overhaul of a corporate culture. He demonstrates perfectly why collaboration should not be viewed only as a program, and therefore the focus should not be centered only on external operations or activities."
Dennis Hammonds, Managing Partner, Heritage Logistics Group, LLC

Creating A
COLLABORATIVE
ENTERPRISE

*How to retool your organization to
dominate your markets*

R O B E R T L . N I T S C H K E

BOOK PUBLISHERS NETWORK

Book Publishers Network
P.O. Box 2256
Bothell • WA • 98041
Ph • 425-483-3040
www.bookpublishersnetwork.com

10 9 8 7 6 5 4 3 2 1

Printed in the United States of America

LCCN 2010903921
ISBN10 1-935359-34-7
ISBN13 978-1-935359-34-0

Cover designer: Laura Zugzda
Typographer: Stephanie Martindale

This book is dedicated to my wonderful bride Barb, who has always been my best friend, partner and key supporter; to my children: Shawna, Carrie, Rob and Tracey; and, especially, to my heart-grabbing grandchildren: Cody, Mikayli, Paige, Aunika, Amber and Abigail.

CONTENTS

ACKNOWLEDGEMENT

The Concept of the Collaborative Enterprise (CE) started with an article describing the attributes of the CE, written over a year ago. It was the prompting of associates and friends that encouraged me to expand the topic to include suggested changes an organization could make to become more collaborative. Further encouragement led me to the publishing of *Creating a COLLABORATIVE ENTERPRISE.* A special thank you to Al Eaton, Terry Stavrouplos and Dick Hol for their long time friendship, unbias comments, suggestions and contributions. To Carl Levi, PowerProof, LLC, who edited, educated and patiently molded the text into a readable form, I am very grateful. To the entire team of professionals at Book Publishers Northwest, and especially Sheryn Hara; thank you for your interest, respect and guidance through the publishing process. A very special thank you to my wife Barb, who spent many hours reviewing and applying her professional business skills in support of the final version of Creating a COLLABORATIVE ENTERPRISE.

# INTRODUCTION

There is a new organization that is evolving and beginning to dominate markets in a number of different industries, and the people involved are not aliens or graduates of a new organizational development think tank. Until you look more closely at how they operate and act, most of these individuals look just like those in your organization. However, they are different and they are very, very good at what they do. One thing is certain; they are going to dominate your market sometime in the future.

There are volumes written about organization development and the positives and negatives of various implementation methodologies.

After more than thirty years of business experience across several industries and different-sized companies, I have concluded that the successes and failures of most organizations are due to their culture, which is relatively unknown to their executive management and owners. Management is focused on creating strategies that, if fulfilled, generate results that will create increased value for the organization they serve.

The ways they go about their business are usually a reflection of their experience, skills, goals and objectives and the response of the markets they are addressing. All too often, the leaders do not take into account the attributes of their culture and the impact it has on the effectiveness of their company. More and more progressive leaders understand this fact and are beginning to rework their cultures into well-tuned machines that are beginning to appear as corporations that are significant challengers to their competition.

The term *Collaboration* seems to be the new buzz word in business circles. It is used most often in the same context as *cooperation*, and yet it actually implies so much more.

I see *Collaboration* as the launching pad for a growing number of organizations which are tackling the daily challenges by assembling existing methodologies. These methodologies are then used in a much more direct and simplified way, achieving outstanding results.

Such organizations, which I refer to as *Collaborative Enterprises or CEs,* have the capability of dominating their markets - and possibly entire industries. The *Collaborative Enterprise* knows how to assemble the strategies, tactics and execution techniques and then how to muster the resources that set it apart from its competition. Are these techniques new? No! Are they revolutionary? No! Are they effective? Yes!

This book started out as an article; but, through the encouragement and prompting of colleagues and friends, it has taken on a much more serious intent. My passion is for seeing the expansion of the *Collaborative Enterprise* operating culture into more American industries. This enthusiasm has led me to introduce you to this new type of organization, its attributes, the reasons for its success and how to change your company to achieve a similar level of success.

I hope that your eyes will be opened to the strategies, tactics, tools, and techniques that are available to you so that you can begin *Creating a Collaborative Enterprise and retool your organization to dominate your markets.*

SECTION ONE

What Is a Collaborative Enterprise?

 WHAT IS A COLLABORATIVE ENTERPRISE?

The Collaborative Enterprise (CE) is a philosophy that is emerging within the worldwide business environment that has the potential for revolutionizing corporations' cultural values and how these organizations perform.

The Collaborative Enterprise did not evolve out of a new organizational development technique or business managerial concept. Instead, it has emerged in response to the ever-growing need to increase the speed to market for products and services, the demand for the delivery of those products and services at the highest level of quality and the lowest possible cost, and the need for the enterprise to accomplish all this within a revolutionary open-operating environment with *all* of its stakeholders. These stakeholders include the organization's entire workforce, customers, ownership, vendors/suppliers, community, Governments, and competitors. We will discuss each of these entities in greater depth in a later chapter. The *key* identifier of a Collaborative Enterprise is the successful way it can relate to and support all of its stakeholders who are essential to the accomplishment of the organization's mission.

The Collaborative Enterprise does not exist in only one industry, nor is it limited to certain types of products and services. The CE is characterized by a corporate philosophy promoting a customer-centric focus and a self-balancing, integrated, operating structure that is sometimes called an ecosystem. This unique structure enhances the delivery of products and services in an open-communications environment that promotes the collaboration of all stakeholders in meeting the corporation's objectives.

By lowering the functional and political walls and reporting fences of the traditional organizations, this new approach provides the structures and operating emphasis needed to accommodate the effectiveness and efficiencies that are the foundation of a CE.

The over-burdening compliance processes and constraints found in most enterprises today are replaced in the CE model by relevant controls and monitoring activities that provide real-time, value-based information which immediately converts into increased efficiencies and effectiveness of the Enterprise.

The CE framework is a philosophy, but it requires all the same, basic operational aspects of any effective organization; the CE simply positions its operational activities and resources under a new environment, which results in producing greater benefits to the Enterprise, both directly and indirectly.

My objective is to provide you with the guidelines needed by any organization considering making changes in their way of doing business and who are considering taking the next step toward renovating their organization so that they can better compete in their markets.

The numbers of Collaborative Enterprises are growing in all markets across the world and certainly within the United States. If your company is not considering a change in the way you conduct business, I am certain that you will be competing with a Collaborative Enterprise sometime in the foreseeable future.

To effectively compete, you first must know the competition. Therefore, let me introduce you to my view of the *Collaborative Enterprise* and what makes it so special. After reading this book, if you decide that the Collaborative Enterprise environment is not for you, at least you will be aware of the key factors that the CE competition will be using to capture your customers and employees.

Key Pieces:

- Create an operating philosophy to improve the speed to market using increased levels of quality, lower costs and customer-centric organizations.

- Emphasis on the importance of collaborating with all stakeholders to meet company mission.

- Renovation of the corporation by evolving its practices to lower encumbrances, allowing open, real-time communication; value-based information; relevant controls and strong leadership.

- There are no industry or market constraints for the Collaborative Enterprise. Are you ready to compete with them?

SECTION TWO

Who Are They?

Where Are They?

Why Are They Superior?

# WHO ARE *THEY*?

They are organizations found in any industry, from manufacturers of durable goods to the high-technology, clean rooms of the chip makers. *They* are software companies, construction companies, bio-technology companies, international consulting organizations, and grocery store chains. *They* are the mega-million-dollar non-profit charities, research think tanks, and private educational organizations. *They* represent the holders of a vision that has boundaries but is limitless in terms of their drive to improve. *They* are existing organizations that have been operating under the traditional view of organizational management practices for decades. *They* are also the new, early-stage entrepreneur-driven entities that have not yet experienced the pressing challenges of maintaining customer loyalty but who will do so soon — and it will be either very exhilarating or extremely devastating.

The Collaborative Enterprises or CEs are all led by a framework of leadership that is difficult to chart, due to its depth and breadth within the organization. Titles won't help, because most are transparent and of little value, other than to describe the title-holder's expertise.

These are organizations that are not very visible within their industry, and their leaders prefer it that way. They are often not recognized; but, if they are, it is most often for their outstanding performance, rather than their public-relations campaign — a prop they don't need.

Their leaders are just that, leaders – highly-motivated, operational visionaries, committed to their industry and embracing accountability, maintaining an unwavering focus on execution and believing in the internal growth of expertise. They are highly-compensated, as they should be; but, usually they are not driven by personal wealth. A CEO recently shared this point by saying, "*In all my years of employment, I have enjoyed many bonuses; however, I would have done the exact same job WITHOUT them. The Financial reward of a bonus simply does not stimulate the individual, as most people believe it does.*"

They are the organizations that understand how quality hiring, augmented by continuing education of their employee base, produces a motivated, flexible and highly-skilled workforce. They put their action ahead of rhetoric when they say, *Our people are our greatest asset.* They take great pride when an employee leaves for greater opportunities, because they know that they have provided that individual the environment that enabled him/her to excel and prepare for new opportunities, whether internally or externally. I have been asked many times, "How do you deal with problem employees?" I usually answer, "By not hiring them in the beginning."

They are the organizations that embrace an open society within their structure. They see real-time, open communication as one of the keys to their increased momentum and success. Their stakeholders certainly appreciate this commitment to communications and how it creates an advantage for each of them to increase their performance and better control their operating risks. A Collaborative Enterprise is truly an ecosystem, with each of the organization's stakeholders taking a position at the table of influence and working in a committed partnership. Who are *they*? *They* are an organization that knows it needs to operate within a new framework in order to survive and excel in the future. Just watch your industry and you will find them. They are the organizations that are taking your market by storm, eroding your market share, and hiring your best and brightest employees.

Key Pieces:

- They are not bound by any industry or market segment.

- They are established as well as start-up companies that are driven by change.

- Their leaderships are contrarian and execution visionaries.

- Their leaders are not simply driven by personal gain.

- They are stealth organizations that fly under the industry radar until they are recognized for their exceptional performance.

- They know the importance of hiring correctly and investing in their workforce.

- Their operating environment is an ecosystem which includes their stakeholders.

 WHERE ARE THEY?

W here are they? They are everywhere. They are found in every corner of the world and in every thriving or struggling economy. They are emerging out of the recessions, the business cycles and the technology life cycles. They are the organizations that refuse to follow the worn path of the past and present, which is littered with organizational failures, large and small. They see a brighter future if they can change their ways and learn from the mistakes of others. They believe their approach for their company will survive and flourish, and they have every intention of proving it to those who continue to operate their organizations from their rear-view mirrors.

Where are they? Their progress is forever in-process. Some are further along than others, and some don't even know that they are going to join the growing numbers of other Collaborative Enterprises. Most are not plan-driven but reaction-driven. Don't underestimate them; they are organized and extremely focused on their core capabilities and strengths. Most, but not all, are private, younger, smaller, and less experienced. They are all over the world, and they see the global market as the place where they must cohabit and succeed.

I can tell you where they *are not*. They are not in the structures of local, state and federal governments or public institutions, where performance is measured by political leverage, information hoarding, and control — where success is measured by what you accomplished for your special interest group and not for your stakeholders.

The organization that recognizes that it must create — not print or collect from others — wealth for its stakeholders has the greatest potential to beat the odds and become a Collaborative Enterprise. Those that do not make the transformation into a CE will eventually join the ranks of the mediocre or, most likely, those who fail.

Key Pieces:

- They are located internationally within thriving and struggling economies.

- They have a vision that surpasses their surroundings and the way things are.

- The global economy is their marketplace.

- They are committed to the prosperity of their stakeholders.

# WHY ARE THEY SUPERIOR?

The Collaborative Enterprise, or CE, will outperform its traditional organization competition on all levels. Why? Enterprises that have adopted the CE model are not held captive to the Industrial Revolution managerial leadership and control mentality.

The leaders see themselves as pathfinders in the new movement to bring the products and services desired by their customers to those patrons in a manner not accomplished previously, with an unprecedented level of cooperation with their stakeholders.

They know that friction produces drag and heat, which, over time, will break down the structural integrity of a component and cause eventual failure. They know that organizational friction brings about poor communications, unnecessary complexity, waste, delay, increased cost, and lackluster performance when measured from the customer's perspective. The end result is the loss of that customer.

CEs believe they can generate momentum as a multiplying factor when utilizing their resources, i.e., working at getting the greatest benefit from the fewest resources possible, while developing an environment that motivates, delegates and rewards "common sense."

The Collaborative Enterprise is an organization in a state of perpetual motion; its members believe in generating and protecting its positive momentum techniques just as Coca-Cola protects its formula for Coke.

Cultures are what drive organizations to success, mediocrity or failure. Those in a CE know this and pay constant attention to the real-time condition of the organization's culture. The CE keeps an evaluating eye on the impacts of its successes and failures and how their operational environment (ecosystem), which is at their cultural epicenter, is responding on a minute-to-minute basis.

Why are they superior? Simply put, the CE gives its customers what they want when they want it, at the price they will pay and at an unbelievable level of quality — all within an open-operating environment that is repeatable. A significant advantage for the CE is that their customers feel they are a part of the Collaborative Enterprise as true *stakeholders*.

Key Pieces:

- They see their stakeholders as participants in providing their customers with products and services in a superior manner.

- They focus on the impacts on their culture that will supercharge or impede their results.

- They look to eliminate organizational friction and its negative impacts.

- They are in perpetual motion.

- They understand the importance of positive momentum.

- They see their operating environment as an integrated ecosystem and work very hard to keep it in balance.

SECTION THREE

How Did They Start?

What Is Their Strategy?

What Is Their Structure?

Who Is Their Leadership?

Who Are Their Stakeholders?

# HOW DID THEY START?

Until quite recently, if a new organization had the luxury, it would start with a plan – but not a plan that envisioned a Collaborative Enterprise. Typically, the plan was to strategize and execute in a certain manner, knowing that those contrarian approaches were needed to set the Enterprise apart from the other hunters looking to increase their share of the overall market.

Most Collaborative Enterprises started their transformations as "Evolutionists." Although established as traditional organizations with industry-groomed ideals and methodologies, they found themselves searching for a "better way." They saw a need for change, either brought about by unsatisfactory performances or other events within their industry or the economy in general.

Over time, these organizations concentrated more on forward-looking strategies and tactics than the trends of the past. They saw a strong need to leap-frog their competitors — choosing to take the risk that they could generate and maintain an "advantage gap" that would be difficult for others to overcome.

The Collaborative Enterprise looks at its goals through longer-term glasses than most organizations. CEs see growth as something that must be sustained, not just gained. They understand that in order to prolong growth, they must have the right operating environment in place. That environment is comprised of a number of factors that will make them more progressive than others. How did they know which factors were the right ones? Most of the time, they didn't.

Most organizations are shaped by trial-and-error or lessons learned. However, what makes CEs more progressive is that they learn much faster. They don't fall back on their old ways when they experience a setback. Instead, just the opposite takes place. They move forward with the same determination and quest for cooperation, speed and results as before. These setbacks have not been failures in their eyes. On the contrary, they were learning experiences. Note the difference in their attitude. Most organizations experiencing failure simply accept it as failure, retreat from their endeavor to the safety of the past and come to an abrupt halt. CEs recognize that a failure is just another obstacle to overcome, and they add it to their list of assets accumulated from lessons learned.

CEs are quick to adapt to new situations and to adopt those strategies and techniques that fit within their overall push for increased performance. You won't find a comment such as, "If it's not invented here, then it's not for us," in a CE. They are adaptable and very flexible. They believe that if there is an existing approach that may help them — but others have tried and failed — they will try it anyway, in the belief that they can do a better job of executing it than others.

Here is a story that illustrates this point. It was about Vincent Lombardi, the famous ex-coach of the Green Bay Packers. Someone asked him why his championship teams were so successful with so few plays. He commented (and I am paraphrasing), "We don't care if they know our plays; if we execute them properly, they still cannot stop us."

CEs look at their operating ecosystem and know that every function and process is intertwined and must be taken into consideration with regard to new products, services and processes. They've created their environment to support the leadership, employees, vendors/suppliers, regulators, owners/investors and, most importantly, customers in a manner that produces the richest results for each of these stakeholders. In turn, the operating environment has evolved into a level of shared accountability, requiring each stakeholder to participate in the process in order to guarantee that the end results of the business processes are efficient and effective.

How did they start? In most cases, they evolved. Why? They wanted to. An organization does not take on a new operating philosophy simply because a new book with a few ideas for making changes has appeared on the best-seller list. CEs are driven to be the best at what they do. What they factor into the "what they do" is *every* aspect of the organization — not just their product development, or research, or sales, or customer care. They know that, like any ecosystem, theirs must be kept in balance to perform optimally; and, when it is out of balance, it will change to right itself. CEs are always in the process of righting themselves. Does this take effort? You bet. Does it take consistent and unwavering commitment? Yes, it does. Does it move them ahead of the competition? Definitely! That is the whole point.

Key Pieces:

- They begin out of a desire for change for the better.

- They are "Evolutionists."

- They want to leap-frog the competition and create an advantage gap.

- They view success over the long term and the ability to sustain their growth.

- They view failure as an asset, which is added to their long list of lessons learned.

- They are adaptive and extremely flexible, but they remain very focused.

- They view their operating environment as an eco-system, composed of their stakeholders; and, for optimal performance, they realize that it must be kept in balance.

 WHAT IS THEIR STRATEGY?

The Collaborative Enterprise has a simple, underlying, organizational strategy: do *what we do better than anyone else and create value for our stakeholders.* Their strategy is to operate more effectively and more efficiently than anyone else. What does that mean? It means that the organization's collective mindset is centered around an operating framework consisting of 5 priorities: (1) produce a product or service needed by the customer; (2) provide the product or service to the customer faster than anyone else; (3) provide a level of quality appreciated by the customer; (4) provide the product or service to the customer at an acceptable price; and (5) create value for their stakeholders (see *Who are Their Stakeholders?*).

The interesting fact about CEs is they know that in order for their strategy to work, the operating framework, which is so critical to their success, must "evolve" into a balanced structure and that it will continue to evolve over time. Up to this point, we have been referring to that balanced structure as an operating ecosystem.

We can try to characterize an operating ecosystem as *a community of operating units which are interactive with, and supportive of, each and every other unit, which has a hierarchy driven by the corporate mission and operating results, and held together by open communications of real-time information, stratified leadership and functioning within a continuous improvement environment.*

Let's simplify this description to better understand this critical factor for the implementation of the CE's overall operating strategy. The CE knows that every function or process within the organization has to interact with - and will impact - every other function in the course of meeting their operational goals. They know that the interaction of the ecosystem includes all their stakeholders. They also realize that these functions need to interact as smoothly and as quickly as the integrated components within a microchip and that their Enterprise — their *microchip* — is powered by open, accurate and real-time communication.

What is their strategy? The CE is focused on the longevity of the organization and the ability to be the best at what they do. In order to maintain their momentum, they know that their environment is influenced by internal and external circumstances that must be addressed. To address these influences in a way that will work to strengthen the organization, it must continually strive to improve.

Nearly every CE continuously attempts to improve every aspect of the organization. This includes the way they view their goals, objectives, products and services, processes, methods, personnel, and the relationships with their stakeholders. It is this strategy that sets them apart from their competition and places them in the position of having the opportunity to nurture a significant following of loyal customers.

Key Pieces:

- Their overall organizational strategy is to be the best at what they do and to create value for their stakeholders.

- Their 5 priorities are to:

  - Produce products and services that the customers need.

  - Provide those products and services to the marketplace faster than the competition.

  - Provide a level of quality appreciated by their customers.

  - Provide their products and services at an acceptable price.

  - Create value for their stakeholders.

- Their operating strategy is built on the concept of an evolving ecosystem.

- They are focused on the longevity of the organization and its overall effectiveness through a mindset of continuous improvement at all levels.

WHAT IS THEIR STRUCTURE?

The Traditional Organization's functional structure — which we are most familiar with — depicted in Figure 1 below, is much more constrained than the Collaborative Enterprise's functional structure, found below in Figure 2.

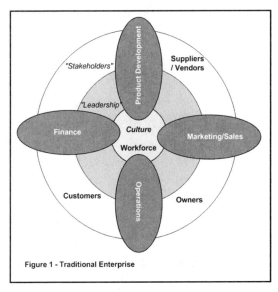

Figure 1 - Traditional Enterprise

A CE has all the same activities required to perform like a traditional organization; it has product development, marketing and sales, finance, operations and leadership for all these functions.

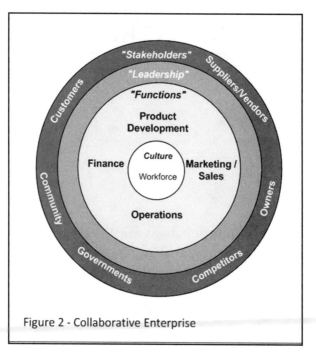

Figure 2 - Collaborative Enterprise

What you should easily see from comparing these functional diagrams is how differently their functions interact with each other. One of the key differences is the commitment of the CE to keep the activity flow between functional operations to a minimum. They look to achieve a much higher degree of integration of functions — as shown without functional separation — than is found in a non-CE organization.

The Collaborative Enterprise's structure has evolved, and is purposely designed, to meet each objective of the overall organizational strategy. For example, the leadership at all levels of the CE is hand-picked for their ability to work within an operating ecosystem environment.

Note: We'll discuss leadership shortly. If you want to jump ahead, you can refer to *Who is Their Leadership?*

The functional organizations within the CE are configured to ensure that they meet the overall strategic objectives of the organization, i.e., speed, quality, functionality, cost and cooperation. Notice that I said the structure was focused on the *overall organizational* strategy, not a departmental or functional strategy.

In an ecosystem operating environment, it is very important that all functions and stakeholders are focused on the organizational strategy and goals. Once an individual function focuses *only* on its individual activities, unit, or department, then the ecosystem begins to get out of balance. There is no room for "I did my job" or "That's not my job" in the CE organization.

Since most CEs evolve over time, it is common to see a traditional organization structure on paper. Yet, the CE organization is well aware of the attributes needed to ensure that it operates as an ecosystem and that they may not have arrived yet at this goal in all areas of operation. In these circumstances, there is nothing wrong with their structure; it's just that they are evolving.

Don't be confused by an organizational chart that may show a traditional structure within a CE. When you observe the overall operation of the CE, you will begin to see the inter-workings of the functions within the ecosystem do not follow the rigid hierarchy of the organizational chart.

What is their structure? Their structure is determined by how far they have evolved. They search for operational efficiency and effectiveness through continuous improvement. They focus on improving communication among all of the organization's units within their environment by providing the accurate, valuable and real-time information required to meet their needs. They integrate functions and operations, improve communications, and shrink infrastructures in order to improve speed, quality, function, and to reduce cost and increase cooperation with stakeholders.

Here is another way to look at the difference: a *traditional company* is in a building that can be viewed as a place where every person inhabiting that building has an office. On the other hand, the *Collaborative Enterprise* is in a building where every person has a desk, but no office — not even a cubicle. The desks are pushed together, so that people can reach out and touch each other and can communicate without any real time delay.

This was presented as an analogy, not a recommended office layout for your organization. It was intended to illustrate a point. I will say, however, that there are examples where the open-office format does enhance productivity.

Key Pieces:

- Their functional structure is very different from the traditional organizations: less constrained, more open, and fewer obstacles for enhanced communication and improved workflow.

- Their operating structure is designed to meet the overall strategy of the organization and not specialized to any one person, unit or department at the expense of the others.

- They are evolving. Therefore, their organizational structure (organization chart) may look like the traditional organization; but when you look at their "functional" structure, they are becoming an operational ecosystem.

 WHO IS THEIR LEADERSHIP?

The Collaborative Enterprise knows that it is the leadership that provides the direction and the consistency required for the CE to evolve and perform to meet the organization's goals and objectives.

For those who do not yet fully understand the inter-workings of the CE organization, what is confusing is that there is a more ambiguous line of separation for leadership.

There are high levels, medium levels and low levels of leadership. You may say, "The same levels of leadership exist in my traditional organization, too." I say, "You may have the levels of leadership by title, but I bet you don't have them in terms of functionality, responsibility and accountability."

You see, the CE looks at leadership differently than most traditional companies. They identify leadership as the act of leading at all levels of the organization — not just leading from the CEO or another C-level position, while everyone else in a leadership position, who mostly just have a title, seem to follow along. CE leadership at the highest level has tremendous respect and trust for the leadership at the lowest level within the organization and vice-versa. All leaders see themselves as partners with the entire workforce within a CE, and with the stakeholders in general.

This is much different from the demand-and-control leadership style found in the traditional organization. The leadership approach of the CE is one of its cultural traits that truly set it apart from the traditional organization. If the CE is operating under the ecosystem hierarchy, then it knows that each unit must have its own leadership, since there are no kings or dictators within the ecosystem.

Leadership within the CE is hired, trained, mentored and groomed in the traits and skills needed to keep the momentum moving within the organization. All levels of leadership are cognizant of their need to improve and hone their skills to ensure their success in meeting the never-ending challenges and opportunities they encounter. CE leadership believes in the motto: "Our people are our most valued asset."

Any organization knows that in order to be effective and efficient at the same time, it must have a skilled and motivated workforce. In the CE, leaders at all levels are not the overseers of the operation. Rather, they are the supporters of the organization. Do they take responsibility for establishing goals and objectives, track results and provide direction? Yes, they do! It is *how* they do it that sets them apart.

The leaders support the strategies, goals and objectives of the organization; and they see their unit's contribution to those overall directions as key to the success of the entire organization, not just the key to the success of their own unit or function. They see themselves as *coaches or mentors* to their workforce, not as dictators or overseers. Also, they are willing to roll up their sleeves and take a helpful position within their process or function, if necessary. They hold themselves as accountable for their own performance as they do their worker-partners.

The true test for a leader, at any level, is how he/she is viewed by the workforce he/she supports. If leaders are *respected*, then they are doing well. If they are *disrespected or feared*, then they have failed.

Who is their leadership? The leadership comes from those individuals who believe that there is a new way to conduct commerce or serve within non-profit organizations. They have seen the results of traditional organizational structures with walls, elitist leadership styles, workforce-churn techniques, segmented planning, ineffective product development and customer indifference. They know that, in the right situation, they can make a difference. They search out those situations; and when they secure a position, they begin the evolution process.

Developing such leadership takes time, patience, strength, persistence and commitment. I am not talking about just the Chief Executive Officer; I am talking about any level of leader. Although Collaborative Enterprises may evolve faster if the top leadership is fully committed to a CE format that is not the only way to morph into a CE. It can happen from the bottom up. It is all about leadership and generating results that support the mission of the organization, no matter what level of the organization the individual may currently be leading.

Key Pieces:

- Their leaders come to the CE believing in a new way to lead.

- They see leaders at all levels within the organization and treat them all with the same respect.

- Their leaders lead by example and cooperation (delegate and coach), not as dictators or overseers (demand and control).

- Their leaders possess a high level of mutual respect and trust for all levels of leadership and the workforce.

- Their leaders are supporters of the workforce and see that workforce as their most valued asset.

- They hold themselves accountable for their actions, just as they do others.

- Their leaders come to the organization to make a difference and do it in a new way—through real leadership.

WHO ARE THEIR STAKEHOLDERS?

The Collaborative Enterprise has the same list of stakeholders as the traditional organization, but the CE has a different view of who their stakeholders are and the value each contributes to the overall strategic achievements of the organization. Furthermore, the CE is different in how they interact with those stakeholders to achieve their results.

The CE looks at their stakeholders as partners. In that partnership, the CE and each stakeholder have certain responsibilities and hold each other accountable for their results, all of whom are focused on achieving the objectives of BOTH the CE *and* the stakeholder.

Do you see a difference here? The CE actually believes that it is partially responsible for the success of its partners, the stakeholders, just as it believes that the stakeholders are partially responsible for its success. This mindset is one of the core principles of the Collaborative Enterprise and one of the key elements that set it apart from the traditional organization.

Collaborative Enterprises may differ from one another in the industries they represent, the type of products or services they offer, and the geographic locations of their markets; but, they all have the same types of stakeholders whom they consider their partners.

Two critical factors that tie the stakeholders to the CE are the requirement for open and real-time information exchange between the CE and all the stakeholders and earned trust. Partnering with stakeholders does not happen overnight. Remember, CEs evolve. Stakeholder partners require trust and integrity and a lasting relationship so that the sensitive information can be shared, without concerns for losing it to the competition or self-serving individuals.

The CE team knows to use caution and prudence when setting up first-time relationships. They are usually very diligent in their vetting of their relationships, where possible. The following stakeholder descriptions are representative of the average Collaborative Enterprise:

Workforce

The Collaborative Enterprise states with a great deal of commitment, "Our workforce is our greatest asset," and they back that statement up in their day-to-day operating practices.

The striking difference from the traditional enterprise is that they hand-pick their workforce. Moreover, they provide the best tools, techniques and resources possible for the workforce to perform at a high level, including the best possible communication techniques for providing real-time, high-value information to all levels of the organization.

They provide their workforce with the training and mentoring necessary to perform their missions at a high level, and the workforce does not shy away from the responsibilities and accountabilities that accompany their functions within the CE.

Occasionally, the CE provides its workforce the opportunity to own a piece of the CE through stock participation programs. In some cases, the CE is an employee-owned organization, similar to United Airlines, CH2M Hill, Graybar and Round Table Pizza. Are these companies CEs? Some may be and some we know are not. Those that "may be" could be in some evolutional stage of *becoming* a CE. One indication that they do have a CE focus, regardless of what evolutionary stage they may be in, is that, to some degree, a strategy exists that becoming an employee-owned company may generate a greater loyalty and motivation for a higher degree of performance. This is true if the employees are able to participate in the upside of such actions.

CE-focused companies do not always succeed. If your experience with the service or product from one of these or another employee-owned company has been less than satisfactory, keep in mind that the designation of "employee-owned" does not necessarily imply they are *still* in their evolution. They may have stalled or terminated their quest to become a CE.

When we say that the CE workforce is hand-picked, we mean just that. The CE knows that the most important factor in having a motivated and skilled workforce is making a quality hire at the outset. The CE takes the time and involvement of all those interacting with the vacant position to ensure that the candidate selected will fit with the organization's culture and the functional surroundings and has the appropriate skill level to be immediately productive. There is no *sink-or-swim* mentality in a CE for the new hire, such as is found in many traditional enterprises.

There is a commitment to success for both the CE and the new hire, and the evidence is seen in the level of acclimation to their new position, continual training and ongoing mentoring. You may hear something like, *"I want to introduce our new associate, Carrie (fictitious person). We are really pleased that she has chosen to be a part of our organization. Carrie, these are fellow associates you will be working with. We were just discussing (topic of discussion) and we would really appreciate your thoughts."* There is no sink-or-swim, but lots of responsibility and accountability, with clear channels of help or assistance when needed.

The buddy system and self-directed teams are very evident in the CE. If you ask a CE associate what she likes most about working within a CE, you're likely to hear this: *"They explain in detail what they want, they provide me the tools to do it, and they expect me to get it done when I said I would. Then they provide me valuable feedback when I do well — or not. What more can you ask?"*

Whether a CE is an employee-owned CE or not, there is no way to overstate the value of a well-disciplined, motivated and skilled workforce.

The employee's pride in working for a CE is often considered a greater payback to the employee than his financial compensation or benefits. Such employees appreciate that their organization's culture is evolving into one that respects its employees at all levels within the organization and that it knows they are critical to the CE's success.

There will be occasions when the hiring process or employee development process does not function as either the CE or the employee had planned. In those cases, the CE treats the employee with respect and fairness, while acting swiftly to correct the situation and move forward.

Not many CEs are unionized, because there is no need! No matter what function or at what level they participate, the employees are generally satisfied with the way they are treated, compensated and that they are an integral part of the organization. They know they are regarded as true stakeholders and they respond accordingly.

Customers

Customers are the reason every commercial organization exists. No customers, no enterprise.

Most business publications reference customers as stakeholders of organizations and state the importance of knowing the customers' needs and locations.

Collaborative Enterprises take this notion to a new level; they enlist their customers to join their partnership. That's right; they actually incorporate the customers' thoughts, ideas, complaints, and feelings into the entire functioning of the enterprise. I am not just talking about product development. I am talking about all the functions, e.g., marketing/sales, operations, finance, and the impact on all the other stakeholders. To develop this focus and then maintain it does not happen overnight. It takes a concerted effort.

The Collaborative Enterprise characteristically provides products and services that are made-to-order or on-demand, rather than those made for stock or, as we often hear of, a Field of Dreams Approach — "Build it, and they will come." This difference denotes a "pull" strategy rather than a "push" strategy, as represented in Figure 3.

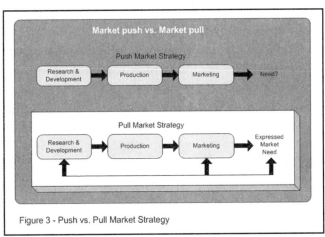

Figure 3 - Push vs. Pull Market Strategy

The customer has input into the designs, features, functionality, quality and even pricing of the product or service. From a product-development viewpoint, this *pull strategy* does not have to be a make-to-order or on-demand product in every case. If you are working under the assumption that there are many potential customers who have the same need for the product or service you provide, then the strategy is to cultivate those customers by getting them involved in the product-development process.

Some companies use focus groups: small groups of customers that generate design ideas, test designs, prototype products, or provide general feedback through surveys. *If*, and that's a big *IF*, the focus group is truly representative of the CE's customer base, then the strategy for using that sample group as a customer stakeholder is an acceptable method. However, if the focus group is made up of partisan, existing customers or *friends* of the organization, then that group is not an adequate stakeholder representative.

From the product marketing, sales and delivery viewpoint, the *pull* strategy is the favored approach for the CE organization. Depending on the type of product or service, the degree of customer loyalty and commitment to a product and/or its organization is usually much greater with a *pull* strategy.

Surveying a large sample group of individuals representing a pool of people — within which an organization *presumes* potential customers exist — is a satisfactory marketing technique, but the data collected cannot replace the flesh-and-blood human contact with a customer who is needed to be classified as a stakeholder.

Specifically, two major criteria apply in making the distinction between an ordinary customer and a "stakeholder." A solid customer-stakeholder can be defined as: (1) an existing customer who is impartial to the company and truly represents the views of those in the marketplace with the same needs and desires for a product and service; and (2) a customer who is willing to invest the time and brainpower for the quest of a new and improved product or service for the industry he or she represents.

As with all the stakeholders, the critical factor that links the customer-stakeholder to the CE is the availability of open and real-time communication. It is this communication — and the CE's activities that thrive on the value derived from the interaction with the customer — that is a characteristic of all Collaborative Enterprises.

Ownership

The ownership of the Collaborative Enterprise is most likely similar to that of any traditional organization. There are smaller owner-operator or partnership structures, as well as large, publicly funded corporations with common and/or preferred stockholders.

What makes the CE relationship with the owner-stakeholder unique is the manner in which they communicate and how the information is valued by the CE in its everyday activities.

You will see repeated throughout this book that a critical factor within the CE is the deployment of open and real-time communication, and that goes for the interaction with the ownership or shareholders of the Collaborative Enterprise. They receive, and are solicited for, viewpoints and feedback about the organization's strategies, execution activities, products or services, and interaction with the markets served through their relationship with the management team.

The CE's leadership understands that the ownership is not only an important stakeholder but that their participation in the strategies and results of the CE are germane to the owner's level of support to the organization during the ups and downs of the business cycles.

Shareholders may participate directly or indirectly, from the Board of Directors or Advisory Board to focus groups, depending on their experience, skills, motivation, and size of their Rolodex.

The CE knows that keeping the ownership informed about the activities and plans of the organization is quite a different matter than just publishing Quarterly Form10-Q or Annual Form 10-K reports, and hosting shareholder meetings. Because of their greater level of involvement and strong desire to see the CE succeed, ownership stakeholders will bring a level of accountability to the CE that is not always found in the traditional enterprise.

Are there challenges that are evident with such an open communication channel to and from these ownership stakeholders? Yes, there are challenges, but that is where the quality of the CE's leadership and their experience is such an important asset for these organizations.

The CE leadership, especially the CEO, is not a *may-I* leader who looks to the shareholders or Board of Directors for day-to-day operating instruction. However, they understand that an informed partner is much less likely to take an extreme advisory role in how the organization is performing if that partner understands the strategies and tactics, and receives frequent updates in an open manner. The leadership believes the value of this form of partnership more than outweighs its inherent challenges, and therefore maintains a priority to groom such a relationship.

Vendors/Suppliers

Vendors and suppliers are often considered stakeholders by the traditional enterprise, because they are the sources of materials, labor and content needed for integrating into the enterprise's product or service. Whether a traditional or Collaborative Enterprise, the greater the level of horizontal dependence on suppliers and vendors, the more important they become to the enterprise.

A traditional enterprise's view of a supplier or vendor is often that of being a *necessary evil*. The organization needs the supplier/vendor's products or services, but their approach is to treat these suppliers with contempt and a lack of trust. The design of an effective supply chain management process is, in fact, a CE-endorsed operation. In these well-defined supplier-support systems (another way to say supply-chain management), there is an openness as to what is needed, when it is needed and how much is needed. The more information the supplier has, the more efficiently he/she can meet the needs of the requesting organization and the lower the cost of the product can be while still retaining healthy profits.

The discipline of *"supply chain management"* is based on the conviction that there needs to be a greater level of participation between suppliers and organizations. In manufacturing and logistical companies, the supply chain management process is thought to be a prime example of collaboration. My experience has revealed that even if the traditional organization implements a *supply chain management* process, the traditional enterprise continually treats the vendor as a lower-class provider and constantly pushes the vendors to reduce costs and improve deliveries. This often holds true, whether or not the vendor can make a profit. Should such a relationship come at the expense of the vendor, the traditional enterprise usually remains rigidly fixed upon its objective of maximizing profits. Unrealistic prices, contract terms or delivery times, as well as deficient communication, are all common detriments for the vendor working with a traditional enterprise. These unworkable items are not the attributes of a healthy partnership, nor do they play any part in the definition of a stakeholder that you will find within the CE.

The Collaborative Enterprise's view of its relationship with vendors and suppliers is one of a true partnership. They are thought of as stakeholders because the CE feels it has a responsibility to help its vendors and suppliers to be healthy organizations.

The CE does this by first bringing the vendor into their strategic and tactical planning processes, their product development, and their operating activities. The CE then helps the supplier implement within the vendor organization many of the same successful strategies, tactics, approaches and systems that are deployed by the CE. This partnership approach is accomplished through that open and real-time communications technique I have been referring to as a core feature of a Collaborative Enterprise, extending to the vendors and suppliers, as well as all the other partners.

As mentioned earlier, just because an organization is deploying a supply chain management process, it does not mean they are engaged in a quest to become a CE, or even that they have a partnership relationship with their suppliers and vendors.

In many traditional enterprises, the implementation of a supply chain management program ends up being just a centralized organization, making the same unreasonable demands on the supplier as in the past. The level of collaboration is limited or non-existent.

The use of processes, automated or not, that provide value information from the CE's planning, product development and operations activities for the benefit of the CE, the suppliers and vendors is a CE attribute. The disseminated information to the suppliers and vendors in real-time or close to real-time, is a key factor that provides the suppliers the best chance to deliver products and services at the appropriate time and cost. The Collaborative Enterprise takes this supply chain management process to a new level, by making an investment in its suppliers and by providing assistance to make sure its "partners" and their partners are successful.

A Collaborative Enterprise may take a bold move and make the relationship with the supplier or vendor an exclusive arrangement. This pact shows the commitment the CE has to the vendor and their suppliers and vendors within the supply chain. There is, of course, a risk in any exclusive relationship. However, in this arrangement, the CE is an active partner and already has the vendor relationship established and the expertise to keep the supply chain partners interactive, integral and healthy.

Community

Looking at the community as a stakeholder is not a common occurrence. Corporations are involved in their communities when it comes to charity events and sponsorships — athletics, arts, Junior Achievement, etc. However, most do not see the community as a stakeholder in their organization.

In a later chapter, I'll discuss how the Collaborative Enterprise views the community, but it is safe to say that the community is a key resource for the provision of many of the infrastructure, services, labor force and local supplier needs for each of the company's possible locations. The CE knows that it is extremely important to keep the community involved with the company and the company engaged with the community.

Governments

The Collaborative Enterprise sees the local, state and federal governments as part of their stakeholder network. These governments, in turn, see all enterprises as a part of their stakeholders. After all, the enterprise, CE or traditional, is a significant tax revenue source for these local, state and federal governments.

The government looks at the enterprise, no matter its size, as a significant contributor to public treasury, from which programs are funded to support the services and security measures obligated by the state and federal constitutions. At the same time, the enterprise looks to the government for those services and protections to assist them in keeping their operations active.

The size and level of success of an enterprise will determine which of these services they will need. Moreover, the CE is actively engaged in their government's issues, including regulation, economic development, service agencies, association partnerships and many grassroots programs which merge the efforts of the public and private sectors.

The Collaborative Enterprise does not see their relationship with the local, state and federal governments as a one-way street. They know they must invest resources to maintain a working relationship with governmental agencies that may have a direct or indirect impact on the CE's business strategy. These interactions may be with enterprise personnel or through lobbyists, who present positions to all levels of government on behalf of the enterprise, either traditional or CE.

If these actions can create benefits to the enterprise for favorable opportunities to win government contracts or receive positive results from regulators, the CE knows that the government is truly a stakeholder and must be nurtured to support its objectives.

Competitors

You might ask, "How could my competitor possibly be a stakeholder?" The objective of the traditional enterprise usually is to clobber its competition into submission or to put them out of business. To make sure, they attempt to beat them in all phases of their business strategy.

The Collaborative Enterprise looks at competitors differently; because, they know that without competition, there may not be a market. There are very few examples of monopolies in the world today. As a matter of fact, they are frowned upon by most governments and economists. Many governments have passed laws to prevent the establishment of monopolies, or for companies to use unfair business practices that may put them into a monopolistic position. Fair and equal competition promotes better markets, yielding more products and services, higher quality, and better pricing. The Collaborative Enterprise sees their competitors as worthy opponents. For the purpose of improvement, they view the competition as an entity to measure themselves against. The CE sees their competitors as industry builders and believes that their cohabitation is good for the industry. After all, it can be said that what is good for the industry is good for the organizations which make up that industry.

The CE is extremely competitive and has a strong commitment to be the best in their industry, leaving the competition in the *dust*. However, the CE does not want to win at the horrific expense of their competitor.

There is a subtle distinction here. You will see the CE involved with their competitors within industry associations, and partnering, when it comes to issues that may be threatening to their industry.

A CE will even help a competitor where there is an issue that may render the competitor unhealthy, such as providing parts to keep a competitor's operation moving, sharing transportation services during slow operating periods, or sharing storage facilities with a competitor to reduce joint operating costs. These are just a few examples.

CEs are not enemies of the competition. Rather, they are just focused on being the best they can be and achieving their goals, but not at the expense of their competition. The Collaborative Enterprise knows that it's better to have a small piece of a larger market than a larger piece of a much smaller market.

Note: By the list of stakeholders I have just described, you can see that, in the long run, the Collaborative Enterprise has a holistic view of the partners that it needs to be successful. The CE's leadership is far advanced of their traditional organization counterparts, because these traditionalists have no clue as to the value *of* and the responsibilities that are needed *for* maintaining true, stakeholder partners.

Key Pieces:

- They understand the importance of grooming stakeholder partners to support their long-term strategies.

- They identify many more stakeholder partners than the traditional organization, which leads to their greater success.

- Their stakeholders are the following:

  - Workforce
  - Customers
  - Ownership
  - Vendors/Suppliers
  - Community
  - Governments
  - Competitors

- They know that each stakeholder has a different set of needs and, in return, provides a critical part of their success puzzle. They work diligently to maintain positive relationships with each group.

SECTION FOUR

How Do They Operate?

HOW DO THEY OPERATE?

The Collaborative Enterprise operates on the premise that the *manner in which it conducts business is just as important as what it produces.* It is always looking for ways to improve its operations in order to meet its organizational strategies. The Japanese call this philosophy of continuous improvement, "Kaizen", and it is a cornerstone for the Lean manufacturing methodology. I would summarize *Lean manufacturing* as a philosophy of engaging in ongoing activities to reduce waste and flow time from manufacturing processes.

I have outlined most of the characteristics of a CE in the earlier sections of this book, and now it is appropriate to spend a little time exploring how their actions are influenced by these characteristics.

As mentioned earlier, the Collaborative Enterprise operates on the ecosystem framework. The CE knows that in order for the ecosystem to perform in balance, the components must work in unison, not in conflict. The self-balancing mechanism within the CE ecosystem depends on the combination of open, real-time communication, a skilled and committed workforce, and a talented leadership that knows how to direct from the sidelines, allowing the workforce to take responsibility for the work at-hand and self-impose accountability for the results. Along with these characteristics, the CE may use a flexible process model to address its projects and issue resolution and activity analysis.

The CE operates through this flexible process model that is deployed within all functional areas of the enterprise. This model takes into account the existence of open communication, self-directed qualified teams, and a commitment to continuous improvement. The model can be divided into five process steps: (1) envisioning the desired results to be achieved, (2) speculating on the means to achieve the desired results, (3) investigating the acceptability of the options to achieve the desired results, (4) adapting to changes that impact the options to achieve the desired results and (5) achieving the desired results (see Figure 4).

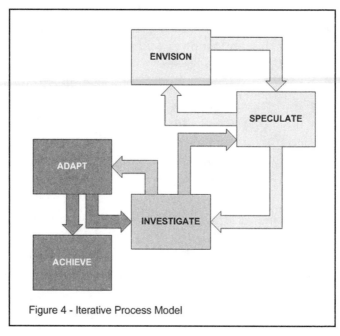

Figure 4 - Iterative Process Model

The teams established to work within the CE process model are comprised of all the stakeholders necessary to have input to the process in order to achieve the desired results for the task being addressed. These five steps are accomplished in an iterative – or repetitive - process which is focused on achieving the desired results as quickly as possible, with the highest level of quality.

The iterative process begins by dividing the task into the smallest number of desired results and then applying the process model to each of these small, individual desired results. Because the process fosters efficiencies in all areas and at all times, it then meets the third strategy of a CE — that of achieving the desired results, at the lowest possible cost. Let's look at each step a little more closely.

Envision

Envisioning the desired results to be achieved means to formulate ideas that have a wide spectrum of options for producing the desired result. The remaining stages or phases of the model are to test the practicality of each of the individual options identified, to finalize the overall desired results to be achieved, and ultimately, to achieve the desired results for each item within the overall task.

If you're in a product development function, the first step is to compile a detailed breakdown of the features, functions, and attributes of a new product or service.

In marketing and sales, the product may be the development of several customer profiles for identifying the potential target of a new marketing campaign to penetrate new markets.

In operations, the product may be a list of actions that should be considered in order to correct a problem impacting the availability of the enterprise network to its customers, which is failing sporadically.

Depending on the nature of the task, the purpose of this envisioning step is to identify what has to be done, at the lowest level, and how it will be accomplished.

This is usually done by a team of CE employees, vendors/suppliers, and leaders that are subject-matter experts and who know the operational aspects of the CE. This team is selected for their individual skills; their ability to work as a self-directed group; and their ability to collaborate with customers, vendors and suppliers, internal operation functions and other stakeholders. The key point here is that they act as a *team*, with no departmental or organizational walls impeding their communication. They function as a group who are unencumbered by any political jurisdiction issues that a traditional enterprise would use to slow down the process while the team waits for approvals from leadership somewhere within the enterprise — and the leadership may have other agendas.

Speculate

Speculating on the approach necessary to achieve the desired results signifies to hypothesize on what the solution(s) may be to achieve the desired results identified in the Envision step.

At this stage of the model, there is insufficient information to identify a clear solution to the desired result of the task at hand; and, this is where the iteration process begins between the Envision and Speculate steps.

Each of the desired results from the Envision step are researched and tested within the Speculate step — to see if it is even practical to proceed with the notion that the envisioned results could possibly be achieved under the current circumstances.

At this step, the potential resources, workloads, risk assessment and estimating of time and cost are analyzed at a high level.

If the desired results seem achievable at this step, with the limited analysis completed, then the process moves on to the Explore step.

If, however, that is not the case, the desired results will be sent back to the Envision step to see if this option can be changed to retain it as a possible solution, which would then be reviewed again by the Speculate stage. If the item cannot be improved at the Envision stage, then it may be dropped as an alternative at this point and other desired results identified in the Envision phase will be explored in the same manner.

If the entire list of potentially desired results to be achieved cannot make it through this Speculate step, then the task must be re-evaluated to see if the overall strategy should be changed to reflect a more realistic and doable task or dropped entirely.

Let's say a product is envisioned to have multiple power sources, i.e., solar, wind, water, etc. The Speculate phase would test the needs in order to support this feature for each of the power source options, as to what would be required to meet that result. Perhaps the process will support all forms of power, or hydroelectric may be eliminated for technical, geographical or application inadequacies.

Another example might be a marketing campaign that has identified several age and gender groups as desired targets. After further review, results produced show an inability to attract males over the age of 45 to their message, while all other gender groups over the age of 25 would be drawn to their message or brand.

As for the network problem, the Speculate process may show that all the alternatives envisioned earlier are viable fixes, and now it must be determined whether or not they can be accomplished, and which is best.

Those desired results that seem to pass muster through the Envision and Speculate steps are then passed on to the Investigate Step. This is done in order to proceed to the next level of review to see if the solutions identified in the Speculate step have the potential for achieving the desired results for the task.

There could be multiple teams, each working on a separate, desired result through all five phases (Envision, Speculate, Investigate, Adapt and Achieve). There could be separate teams that work each phase independently, handing off the results of each phase to the next team. However, having specialized teams is not the most effective way to use the iteration process methodology, since the assumption is that each team has the required cross-functional expertise required to achieve the desired results from start to finish. Once the Envision and Speculate process is completed, it is on to the Investigate step.

Investigate

Investigating the acceptability of the solution to achieve the desired results denotes establishing a clearer understanding of what it takes to complete the task with the desired results.

To accomplish this step, there needs to be a viability test of the assumptions and understandings which came out of the Speculate step.

If the option for accomplishing the task has proven to be valid, now is the moment to move forward with the actual execution of the task. This step includes the planning of the task for completion by managing the workload, resources and appropriate practices necessary to be successful. Execution also involves the firming-up of the team and resources needed to execute the plan, and how they will collaborate with each other.

If the Investigate step proves to invalidate a resource or practice needed to accomplish the desired deliverable for the task, then the team will go back to the Speculate step and re-evaluate another approach to be tested for practicality. If no other options are available, then, as the song goes, "*You got ta know when to hold'em and when to fold'em.*"

If in our example of a product using solar power, the power-generating chip technology is tested; and, it turns out that the solar option of power generation is less practical. Then, the team would go back to the Speculate step to work on other technologies. Any alternate potential solutions would then be sent back through the Investigate step.

Through further investigation, the marketing campaign example may show that it cannot be defined effectively to include both male and female genders and that it needs to be re-evaluated as to where the genders must be split into two campaigns; or, alternatively, is there a way to make it more appealing with a modification to the message? Now the team begins to speculate on that modification as part of the Speculate step.

The network solutions example's options all seem to work in solving the network outage problem, but they all take too long to implement, so the team goes back to the Speculate phase to determine how it can improve the implementation time for any or all of the potential solutions.

The iterative process of going from Envision, to Speculate, to Investigate is best accomplished with the same team working on each desired result. It may require a sub-team of a larger group that includes a number of sub-teams, each working on a desired result, or a single team working on one prioritized, desired result, at a time.

Through the Investigate phase, issues may arise that are not severe enough to warrant a move back to the Speculate step, but they should be evaluated in terms of whether or not to adapt to the new solutions under review. That is why the Adapt phase is very important to the overall process model.

Adapt

Adapting to changes that impact the solutions to achieve the desired results implies that through the iterative processes of Envision, Speculate and Investigate, conditions will arise that may call for the planned solutions to be adjusted. If it is determined that the results can be achieved as planned, once the approved adjustments are made, then the process model takes that into account. The Iterative Process assumes that the planned resources or practices for achieving the desired result may need to be adjusted. That both the team and the enterprise need to recognize that such potential situations may exist.

The more adaptable the CE, the greater the opportunity to move forward with its overall objective, instead of reverting back to the Envision phase and looking for the "perfect" desired result, while failing to deliver the desired result as quickly as desired.

In the example of the power product, the CE may decide that they can release the product much earlier, if they offer it with a wind-power generation feature first, followed with the "hydro", and, eventually, the solar option, as new technologies become available. This puts a useable but possibly temporary product in the marketplace sooner than would be possible by waiting for the full-featured product, to be completed and released.

The example of the marketing campaign may be changed to include a regional deployment strategy, since there was formerly inadequate information to ascertain whether a full national rollout would be a cost-effective approach to generating all the results they may have anticipated.

The network outage solution example would have to be adjusted to incorporate the training of customer service representatives regarding the explanation to be provided to customers asking for billing credits for the outage.

These are all examples of how the teams must adapt to the conditions that will inevitably arise during their preparations for a successful launch of their task, with the desired results envisioned in the first step of the iterative model.

Achieve

Finally, "*achieve the desired results*" does not require clarification, since getting the desired results in the shortest possible time and in the most efficient manner is the overall objective of this process model.

Through the iterative process, the continual efforts on the part of the stakeholders team to explore, review, test, plan, and change until the desired results of the task are acceptable for all stakeholders is the activity that will shine a light on the Collaborative Enterprise(s) within their industries.

The example of a power product involving wind power generation capability would now be in the market with the added benefit of showing the quality, price point and promise of new features to be delivered in the near future. Taking this action of the early release of a partial-featured product, is based on the assumption that the customers *will accept* that option. Taking this action may move the company ahead of their competition; because, it gives the customers exactly what they wanted, either entirely, or through the release of new features as upgrades in the near term.

The marketing campaign example produces the response needed by the enterprise to position their products within their market segments as planned. They are stimulating demand faster than their competition; and, therefore, they are selling product much more effectively. This is because they received market information much faster with a regional rollout, instead of waiting for a full national campaign, which can be positioned for a later and more controlled launch.

The example of a network outage situation was restored much more effectively and timely, while the enterprise was impacted less by having developed a reasonable position on customer credits and an effective explanation ready for customer inquiries about the outage.

It is important to note that using an iterative process may not be the solution for all enterprises. However, for those that have a strategy to be first to market, it is one method that does work. If teamed with effective project management practices and true leadership, it will also produce higher quality results and lower costs. Most of those companies moving to an iterative process may be in some level of evolution toward becoming a Collaborative Enterprise—only time and further change will tell.

Key Pieces:

- They have an operating philosophy emphasizing that it is *just as important to focus on "how" they conduct business as it is on "what" they produce.*

- They have an embedded emphasis on "continuous improvement" for all areas of the organization.

- The self-balancing mechanism (ecosystem) within the CE depends on open real-time communication, a skilled and committed workforce, and talented leadership.

- They have a strategy to bring product to market faster than the completion; many use an Iterative Process Model to accomplish that strategy.

- Iterative Process Model Stages are:

    - Envision-Compile a list of "possible" solutions.

    - Speculate-Test the solutions to see if they have merit. If not adequate, go back to Envision.

    - Investigate-Analyze the requirements to implement a possible solution. If not adequate, go back to Speculate.

    - Adapt-Adjust any *not critical* attributes of a solution to produce a viable solution. If not adequate, go back to Investigate.

    - Achieve-Finalize solution and track results.

SECTION FIVE

What Is Needed to Change?

How Do We Start Renovating?

Retool the Organization's Culture

WHAT IS NEEDED TO CHANGE?

What is needed to change? A decision! Making the decision to become a Collaborative Enterprise is a simple process. First make the decision that a change is necessary and then you start to make the change! Getting to this point is not an easy process; but, unless you do, there will be no purposeful change. Instead, there will be only haphazard events that may produce some level of change. Some will be positive and the rest will probably be negative.

Although any organization can renovate itself from a traditional company to a Collaborative Enterprise, it should be understood that this is not an easy process.

The renovation process involves accepting the fact that cultures change slowly and that planning and operating processes must be improved. There must be an upgrade of the workforce's attitude toward their work and possibly their corporation, a shift in the leadership's view of their functions and how they view the workforce, and a wholesale buy-in to a partnership with all stakeholders. Furthermore, this evolutionary process will probably require the replacement of individuals at all levels, who are not able to adjust to comply with the new direction.

By now, you should have a clearer picture of what a Collaborative Enterprise is and how it operates. Hopefully, this knowledge has also heightened your level of urgency for why your organization might want to make the decision to move toward accepting the attributes of a Collaborative Enterprise and begin the evolutionary process. It is clear to me that those organizations which do not move in this direction will either endure in a perpetual state of mediocrity or they will fail completely. It is that important.

Here are a few quick comments about *what* to do to become a CE: First, recognize that the organization *needs to change* in order to better provide the products and services the customers want, when they want them, at a quality level they want, and at a price point acceptable to the customer. Sound familiar?

Second, get a commitment from the entire list of stakeholders by introducing them to your plans for a change toward a CE framework.

Third, create an evolution plan that shows the functions that you want to change and the order in which they should be changed in order to accommodate your needs.

Fourth, train everyone, and I mean *everyone*, on the desired characteristics of the CE, which we have covered in the earlier chapters. Then, train them over and over and over and over again until everyone can visualize, in their sleep, the framework, characteristics and environment of a successful Collaborative Enterprise.

Fifth, open the communication lines within the organization and begin to trust the workforce and leadership, at all levels, to practice what they have been trained to do.

A *need to know* does not mean, "I will let you know when you need to know." That is the traditional demand and control approach to communicating, not that of the CE. Remember, this is an evolutionary process. Therefore, it will take several years for the culture and operating environment to assimilate the characteristics of the Collaborative Enterprise that you want to see present within your organization.

As the stakeholders see the benefits from being associated with your organization, they will begin to believe in the process and momentum will increase. Remember, you are not throwing a switch and turning all your trade secrets over to your stakeholders. They will earn their way into the roles I have outlined earlier, and their loyalty and performance will win them the advantage of being one of your *trusted stakeholders*. Don't get discouraged by the setbacks. They will occur often. Work through them, while always keeping the overall objective in sight. What is the overall objective? The objective is to be a leader in all your markets through a sustainable organization. That sounds like a reasonable justification for the effort.

When I was younger, my late mother and father used to tell me all the time, "If it was easy, anyone could do it and then it wouldn't be as important, would it?" They were right!

Key Pieces:

- Evaluate your situation, make a decision to change or not. Then, either do nothing or start the change process.

- Introduce your stakeholders to your plans for change and get their buy-in.

- Adjust your leadership style and open up your communication lines within the organization.

- Remember that the renovation process is evolutionary, so change will be slower at some times than at others.

- Don't get discouraged. The benefits far outweigh the challenges encountered along the way.

HOW DO WE START RENOVATING?

If you are now convinced that the Collaborative Enterprise is the type of organization that you would like yours to become, that you are fairly confident that you know *what* the CE is, and that you have a much better understanding of *what is needed* to get there, then the next question you probably have is, "*How do we start renovating* our organization?"

I use the word "renovating" because it should conjure up the image of transforming what you have now into something better. That vision contrasts with starting over on a clean slate — which is seldom possible.

Note that there are multiple ways to reach the goal of developing/becoming a CE. The suggestions I am providing are just that, suggestions. The approaches I am offering are based on my many years of experience, backed by many successes and failures.

The level of success and rate of progression are determined by several factors. The most important elements of achieving success involve the level of commitment of the leadership and stakeholders and the degree of existing dysfunction within the existing culture that must be overcome.

The previous chapter presented the initial thoughts that should be considered for moving the organization from the *consideration* stage to the take-action stage. Strategizing, planning, thinking, and contemplating the change are all necessary activities; but, they are the easiest steps to take.

This is because there are no risks to the organization when planning or contemplating. You haven't made a commitment to act on those strategies or plans, so there is no risk of loss. Once the leadership makes a commitment to implement, then the enterprise will view the tactical activities with a more serious eye.

The following chapters are a discussion of one suggested evolutionary approach for the implementation activities needed to support your becoming a Collaborative Enterprise. If you use your imagination, knowledge, skills and your relationships to move forward with the tactical activities and remain focused on the goal, success is very achievable.

Let's assume, for the remainder of the chapters ahead, that you want to change your organization to evolve toward becoming more of a Collaborative Enterprise. Remember, it doesn't matter which industry you are in or whether you are for-profit or non-profit. The objective is the same.

I believe the following, suggested activities will help guide you to your objective. There is no single, right answer for approaching your advancement. If you identify derivations of my suggestions that you feel are producing superior results, use them. Please let me know what they are, as I am always open to new thoughts and methods.

One word about *best practices:* I am a bit of a contrarian when it comes to using this phrase. I don't believe in "best practices", only in *better practices.* Today's *best* anything is tomorrow's *better* something and possibly the future's mediocre nothing. Voltaire said, "Best is the enemy of Good (or Better)." The gist of the quote is that if you wait for perfection, you miss out on the benefits of having something better. I call that wasted return-on-investment.

CEs understand this process by adopting the "continuous improvement" mindset. What you improve today will reap the benefits tomorrow, just before you improve it again to achieve even higher returns.

Forget about trying to be the *best* and concentrate on being *forever better*.

Key Pieces:

- Renovating your organization means to take the positive aspects of it and help it to evolve into a Collaborative Enterprise.

- There are many approaches for starting your evolutionary process. A few suggestions are offered here.

- The future chapters provide guidelines and suggestions, but don't be afraid to develop your own methods.

- CEs are independent of any particular industry and are for-profit and non-profit.

- Don't get side-tracked by "best practices." Just focus on being "forever better".

# RETOOL THE ORGANIZATION'S CULTURE

Cultures within organizations are similar to those within societies. They can vary greatly and they have significant impacts on the actions and performance of their members.

Cultures evolve over time as a result of the actions of past leaders, members and circumstances. Talk to someone who lived before, during and after the Great Depression. This period in the United States' history may have impacted the social culture of Americans more than any other time, with the exception of September 11, 2001 and times of war. How many Americans today would want to turn back the socio-economic clock to that earlier period?

Look at the changes in today's content of movies and television from the 1950s. Look at the changes that technologies have made over the same 50-plus years. Societal change is taking place all around us constantly; and, yet, most of us cannot tell exactly how or when things changed. We just recognize that they did.

Organizational cultures change in very similar ways. Let's evaluate what you can to do to bring your culture more in line with your new objective — that of being more like the CE environment.

Leadership Role Changes

In your current culture, leadership exists at all levels of the organization. No matter how effective it is, leadership still influences the manner in which the culture reacts to everyday events and conditions. It is the top management leadership (CEO, Managing Director, etc.) and supporting governance members (Board of Directors, Advisory Board, Board of Trustees, etc.) for the enterprise who must make and support the commitment for starting your evolutionary ball rolling. The justifications for such change are probably many, and we have looked at a few in earlier chapters (sustainability, growth, profitability, preservation, etc.).

At this stage of our discussion, let's assume the top-level management leadership has made the decision to move forward and that they have the blessing of their supporters.

The top leadership must be the first to change. A good, initial step is to recognize that the "demand and control" philosophy of management leadership at all levels must be replaced with the "delegate and coach" approach. The top-level management team should be sequestered in an environment conducive to team interaction, innovation and open communications in order to map out their strategy for change. Without an effective strategy, there will be no effective change.

Next comes the Commitment Session. Here is where secondary levels of key management are introduced to the proposed direction and changes established earlier by the top-level management team. CEOs or Managing Directors, make sure you have one-hundred percent buy-in from this level of the management leaders within your organization who are in attendance, when concluding your session and before heading for home. Call it a "commitment session," instead of a strategy session.

The commitment session, lasting several days, will outline the approach, the impacts and the initial list of activities that need to be accomplished immediately. Don't short-change the organization by setting unreasonable expectations that all the session activities can be carried out in one, eight-hour day. Also, don't make the mistake of trying to develop a detailed, tactical plan which outlines every activity that must be done for what you envision as a satisfactory implementation of a Collaborative Enterprise. Remember, we continue to call it an evolution because that is the only way it can succeed.

Map out the first 90 days and work with that. Strategies always precede tactics, so focus on the main areas that you want to change (some suggestions are offered in the chapters ahead) and then outline the approach you plan to take to implement those changes. As any good project manager will tell you, incorporate the goal(s) and the objective(s) for each goal, including time-frames, dates, responsibilities, and results to be measured.

All the management attending the commitment session should be on board, the strategies set and the initial high-level tactics outlined. In your quest to change your culture, what should be a next step to achieving a cultural shift? Get the rest of the workforce management leadership, at all the remaining levels, on board by identifying the *leadership stratification approach,* which is discussed next.

Key Pieces:

- Cultural change should begin at the top; the leadership should be the first to change.

- Replace "demand and control" with "delegate and coach".

- When planning for a change, bring the key leadership together for a "commitment session."

- Don't shortcut the process; it will take more than one day.

- Introduce the concept of leadership stratification.

Leadership Stratification

What is Leadership Stratification? It is the "delegation" part of the "delegation and coach" approach to leadership found in a Collaborative Enterprise. It is the process of identifying leaders, empowering them to make decisions, providing them with the "coaching" or mentoring support to carry out their duties, and then tracking their results. Depending upon the level of leadership dysfunction within your culture, this process may take a long time, or it may be welcomed with open arms and travel like a wild fire.

A selection of leadership qualities, work ethic, and team orientation are some of the characteristics you should look for in your stratification candidates. A word of caution: not all current leaders will make the grade to a stratified, leadership approach. Be prepared for resistance and, possibly, outright defiance. How you handle these situations could be the first test showing how committed you are to the process.

There will be a great deal of testing your resolve along the way. Are you ready to make the hard decision? My experience is that the longer you let a disgruntled manager or employee linger within the organization, the more quickly you bring down the overall performance of his/her area of responsibility and those around them. Address the issue immediately, professionally and with dignity for the person in question, but *do it* and do it *quickly*.

I once had a problem manager who, even after several attempts to counsel, mentor and implement performance improvement plans, I could not seem to rejuvenate them. When I privately informed the manager of his termination, I was actually thanked. That's right, he said, "Thank you." He was frustrated with his performance, hated his job and really did not want to be there, but he did not have the initiative to move on. This termination was the motivation needed to move forward and do what he really wanted to do. I have had similar experiences on more than one occasion.

Once your leadership personnel are defined, it is time to assemble them and share your vision for the CE. Outline the strategy and the initial tactics. Include their involvement along the way. It may put them back on their heels a bit that you are asking their opinions on matters during this process, but that should be a signal that you are serious about the changes you have described.

Reassure them that all the other leaders and supporters are fully committed. Convincingly state that without them the cultural shift cannot happen as smoothly or as timely *but that your commitment is so strong, that it will happen.*

Go to each person, individually, and get a personal commitment to being a part of the team and support for the new direction for the enterprise. If you have a team member who is reluctant or non-committal to the change, then you, and the other leadership members, must convert this person or find a way to help him/her find an ideal work environment in another organization. Additionally, be sure to take proper legal precautions before making such a move.

Having secured commitment from your team of leaders, begin practicing the process of stratification.

Put into practice what you have discussed. Create mentoring sessions, outlining the authorities of each level of the leadership and how they are expected to use those powers for the good of the organization, not themselves. This is not the time to create a bunch of Napoleons. Having selected your leaders well, you should have minimized that impact of expanding the leadership authority throughout the remaining levels of the organization.

Now that the leadership team is informed and starting to function under the new approach, it is time to test the top leadership's commitment by conducting a planning session with the new multi-level leadership team's involvement.

It should be noted that cultural changes have a tendency to drift back to their old familiar surroundings. It is wise for the senior management leadership to test periodically the alignment of the multi-level leadership team to the new approach in order to be certain that all is moving forward, as intended. Having performance goals and metrics that reflect the pursuit of these new leadership stratification tactics would be advisable.

Key Pieces:

- Leadership stratification is the *delegation* portion of "delegate and coach."

- Hand-select the leaders who are most likely to embrace the leadership stratification process.

- Pull the team together to explain the goal for the new emphasis for the corporation.

- Poll each leader individually to make sure he/she is on board.

- Deal quickly with those who are not supportive of the new direction.

- Watch for back-sliding to old cultural habits.

Planning (Strategic/Tactical)

The Collaborative Enterprise's approach to planning is very similar to that of the traditional venture. If they are similar, why explain the process? It is my experience that many organizations do not have a formal planning procedure and their results are impacted. It is important to have a planning process no matter what type of organization.

There are four distinct planning components: the "Mission", "Strategic Drivers", "Tactical Drivers", and "Execution Drivers" that must be addressed for an overall, effective enterprise plan.

The CE has a mission statement, briefly explaining the overall purpose for the organization's existence.

By outlining the longer-term, directional issues to be addressed, the CE establishes a strategic plan, concentrating on the "what" they want to accomplish. They break down the strategies into the tactical issues or events that should be performed to accomplish each strategy. The tactics are the "how," within the planning process, they are going to achieve the strategies. The final component is the execution of the plan by describing what activities and desired results are to be done to satisfy the tactics. Execution is the "doing" part of the planning process.

The CE knows the value of planning, and they usually establish a planning horizon that has a range of two to five years.

They establish their strategies, based on the factors most important to their mission. In most cases, those lines of attack are focused on quality of products or services, time-to-market, cost savings, increasing customer loyalty, and improving internal operations.

The CE establishes their tactical goals and objectives for each of these areas; there may be one or many tactical goals for each strategy.

After setting their tactical goals, objectives are created for each goal. Again, there may be one or many objectives for each tactical goal. As one CEO confided to me about his planning experiences, *"Most organizations cannot handle too many measurable goals, so it's best to keep them to a few key ones — maybe three to four, to make them more manageable."*

Let's clear up any of the possible confusion about the terms "goals" and "objectives". Many people in business use these terms interchangeably; but, in fact, they are very different. Perhaps this quick comparison will give you a better understanding of how to use them in your next planning exercise:

> Goals are broad,
>> Objectives are narrow
> Goals are intentions,
>> Objectives are precise
> Goals are intangible,
>> Objectives are tangible
> Goals can be abstract,
>> Objectives are concrete
> Goals cannot be validated,
>> Objectives can be validated

Goals are the blueprints of the house and the objectives are the construction steps for the house. Goals are the conceptualization of what the house should look like and objectives are the actual steps necessary to produce the finished product.

It is very important to emphasize that goals and objectives must be reasonable, achievable, measurable, designed with timelines, and assigned to persons or groups who are held accountable for the completion of each of the goals and objectives.

Following is a sample outline to emphasize the importance of planning and the steps you might consider for your organization:

Strategy 1: Introduce our product X into the Midwest market.

Goal 1: Grow the market share in the Midwest to 10% by 20XX.

Objective 1: Open 12 stores by the end of year 20XX.

Objective 2: Average store sales of 12 new stores should be $1.2 million by the end of 20XX.

Goals 2: Establish brand name recognition within Agriculture submarket by 20XX.

Objective 1: Establish two marketing campaigns, one rural, one urban by 20XX.

Objective 2: Establish an alliance with two existing leaders in the agriculture sub-market by 20XX.

The Tactical planning process for the CE is also similar to the Traditional Organization's, in that the tactical activities associated with each goal and attached objectives are further defined as to HOW, WHEN and WHERE the goals and objectives will be accomplished.

For Example;

Goal 1: Grow the market share in the Midwest to 10%.

Objective 1: Open 12 stores by the end of 20XX.

Tactic 1: Identify 12 cities for new store openings by February 1, 20XX.

Tactic 2: Establish a staffing plan for each store by April 1, 20XX.

Tactic 3: Assemble a property management team to acquire leases, meeting company specifications for each store by June 15, 20XX.

Tactic 4: Establish grand opening schedule for one store each month over next 24 months, with first store opening August 1, 20XX.

You can see that the process of developing strategies, accompanied by goals and objectives for each strategy, followed by the specific tactics supporting those strategic goals and objectives, finally leads to the specific execution results. The process appears very similar to that of the Traditional Organization.

A key point to any planning process and, especially incorporated into a CE's methods, is: "Plans are not static. They are dynamic and must be adaptable." Situations and conditions change and the organizational plans created to move the company forward must be able to adapt to these changes in order to be effective in reaching their anticipated results.

I can remember a situation when I could not get the attention of other groups to rethink their tactics for developing a product, because the new information I had was not included in the "plan". As a result, one particular product launched twelve months late, because we had to fall back and revise the earlier work to accommodate the new information, which I had presented six months earlier. This was not a good use of resources.

Adaptability does not mean wavering focus; it means that plans should be built with the potential for change in mind and not be cast in stone, as are found in many traditional organizations.

What is different in our company that is now undergoing a renovation? The difference is in WHO is doing the planning. The Traditional Organization normally accomplishes its planning by having the highest leadership level develop the strategies, goals and objectives. These results are passed down, along with instructions to the lower level operating leadership to develop a tactical plan for the implementation of the objectives that have been established. Once completed, the lower level operating team presents that tactical plan to senior management for their approval. This is a common example of "Demand and Control" in action.

The Collaborative Enterprise takes a different approach with the WHO participating in the strategic and tactical planning.

The stratified leadership is involved in both the strategic and tactical side of the enterprise planning process.

There are top-level executives in the room, along with the directors, managers and supervisors of different disciplines, who are all essential to carrying out the strategies and tactics of the company. They have equal contribution authority to the process. They jointly work through the roadblocks and other issues that may appear to derail their goals and objectives, but they do it together and with mutual respect for each other's experiences and skills.

Don't confuse this process with that of a democratic organization. That is not the case. The CEO or Managing Director of the Collaborative Enterprise always has the tie-breaker vote; and, a true leader, knowing how and when to use that power, seldom abuses it. The "Delegate and Coach" process works when it is used properly.

Key Pieces:

- Mission statements reflect the purpose for the company's existence.

- Strategic goals define the *what, when* and *where*.

- Tactical goals define the *how*.

- Execution is the *doing* of the Tactical plan.

- Strategies drive tactics, and tactics drive execution.

- A single strategy goal may have multiple objectives; and, each objective may have multiple tactics, which need to be executed.

- A Plan should include multiple levels of leadership, knowledge, skill and experience.

- Keep focused on the plan, but be willing to adapt to change.

Unwavering Focus

A truly identifiable attribute of a Collaborative Enterprise is its ever-present focus on the situation at hand. It seldom is distracted from its overall mission, strategies, goals, objectives and tactics.

Does adherence to that constant focus require going blindly forward without paying attention to the effects of changes in the industry or the economy? No! On the contrary, the CE is continuously on the lookout for impacts on its plans and directions. Its leaders are extremely proactive. They believe that the enterprise run by looking forward through the windshield is much more responsive to change than the enterprise run by looking backward through the rear view mirror.

The leadership at all levels of the organization is continually meeting with their teams and peers to assess where they are in their planning, execution and anticipation of what lies ahead that may impact those plans. They are likened to the football team who is lined up against the opposition for the next play. Not only is the quarterback calling out signals; each player is looking at what is in front of him, and they are telling their teammates what they see.

For the offense, the purpose for the communication is to make sure the play executes as planned. The purpose for the defense is to find a way to upset the plans of the offense and hold them to no-gain. You won't hear, for long, comments like, "It's not my job" or "Let them worry about that" in a CE organization — or on a football team.

An analogy I use often that explains how focus and flexibility can co-exist within an organization is a mental picture of a freeway. You are driving down a four-lane freeway on your way to visit Grandma Alice.

You know the freeway will take you there and you are focused on staying on the freeway. However, a slow-down in your lane is beginning to make you impatient. The lane on your right is moving much faster, so you change lanes. This may happen several times on your way to visit Grandma Alice.

Have you lost focus when you change lanes? Not at all! You are still on the freeway and still going to arrive at Grandma Alice's, as planned.

However, if the slowdown happened in all lanes of the freeway and, in your impatience, you took the nearest exit ramp to find a way around the slowdown; you may have just lost your focus. It all depends on how familiar you are with the territory and where the next entrance to the freeway is located. Watch out for the off-ramps. There may not be another entrance for a long time, and that can be costly!

Key Pieces:

- There is an unwavering focus to detail.

- Be continually on the lookout for impacts and opportunities.

- Manage by focusing through the windshield, not the rear-view mirror.

- Be proactive and adaptable.

- Leaders confide with teams, continually assessing their situation and coaching them to optimal performance.

- Keep team dynamics strong and members involved.

Setting Priorities

The setting of priorities brings about two, very important benefits: it strengthens the organization's focus and it makes efficient use of enterprise resources. A Collaborative Enterprise has a strong drive for efficiency, translating into fewer resources required and lower costs. However, if done incorrectly, prioritization can be misleading and even harmful to an organization.

Many leaders have a priority scheme of 1s, 2s, and 3s, with 1s having the highest priority and 3s having the lowest. Their mistake is classifying almost every event or activity as a 1, and their justification is that all the 1s are important and have to be done first. The question then becomes: which one of the 1s gets done first? Who decides on the order of the 1s? Is every 1 really equally important to the enterprise as all the other 1s? I don't think so.

Priorities derive from a justification process that should be conducted by all levels of the enterprise involved in the identification activity.

Involved and experienced leaders and associates evaluate which of the positive or negative activities has the greatest impact on the organization and then arrange those activities in order of importance.

They use a justification process based on several areas, e.g., resources, cost, time, and future impacts. Once the justifications have been agreed upon, the activities are *ranked*. Ranking is a means of prioritization, but it is based on the fact that no two activities have the same level of impact on the company. Instead of a bunch of 1s, a few 2s and a few 3s, the CE has a number 1, a number 2, a number 3, a number 4, and so on. Maybe numbers 1 and 2 can be worked on simultaneously, but they still have a different level of importance to the company; and, the team has acknowledged that, with the *ranking* of number 1 and 2 for the two events or activities.

Organizations without priorities that are ranked are like sailing ships without a rudder. The ship glides along smoothly and quietly, but it also moves aimlessly, with no ability to change direction.

My personal experience with implementing a ranking-priority scheme is that top management leadership has the greatest difficulty accepting this approach. Your CE leaders understand it, but traditionalists don't. They want everything done now, fearing that any priority lower than number 1 will not get done. Their concern is that anything not done immediately will reflect on their competence, as it should. Unfortunately, they are shooting themselves in the foot with that rationale; because, if they do *not* have a ranking system, they increase their probability for failure to complete the really important events or activities.

Key Pieces:

- Rank the activities in a priority sequence (1, 2, 3, etc.), and not all with the same priority.
- Priorities aid efficiency and proper resource allocation.
- Priorities improve communication and direction.
- Key executives are often the challenge to accepting ranking of priorities.

Engage the Workforce

The workforce is the heart of any organization, and the Collaborative Enterprise recognizes that fact and places its personnel at the top of its list of Stakeholders. It recognizes that the workforce is their most valued asset, a fact we have considered before.

When I talk with organization leaders and owners, I usually hear that they have a healthy commitment to their workforce, yet there is always a "but", which is followed by a diatribe, describing their employees as ungrateful, hostile, argumentative, uncooperative, lazy, etc.

How do you engage a workforce under those conditions? My first inclination is to question the degree to which these conditions really exist across the *entire* workforce. At all levels, every organization has its problem employees. However, Human Resource professionals I have talked with say that "most" employees want to perform above average and contribute to a positive work environment.

Let's explore seven key factors for engaging the workforce on your journey to evolve into a CE:

Factor #1: Hiring

Hire the personnel who are most likely to be successful and who will contribute to the positive achievements of the Collaborative Enterprise. You have plenty of work ahead of you by convincing existing employees that your CE migration process will make their work environment more rewarding.

Fill new positions with enthusiastic individuals who see the opportunity to join such an enterprise as a positive situation. Look for work ethic, communications and interpersonal skills, and core abilities needed to perform the position. Then, get the workforce involved in the hiring process.

Human Resources and Management should not have a monopoly on who gets hired. Are they important in screening candidates to insure they meet the minimum requirement? Absolutely! However, let members of the team who will be working with the candidate have *some* say in the process. After all, they will be making decisions and taking action together, which will make or break the processes for which they are all responsible.

By hiring the individuals who will compliment the CE environment, you render the evolution process a little less complicated. However, if you make a bad hire and find that a candidate is not compatible, as anticipated, then that situation should be dealt with sooner, rather than later.

As previously mentioned, there is no benefit to the employee or the company by prolonging the agony of allowing a poor performer to impact fellow workers and the results of the organization. This is true no matter what the level of the position they hold. Poor performance is a cancer that will impact any organization, if given enough time.

Factor #2: Training

If any organization wants to develop a skilled and flexible workforce, there must be an understanding of the value that continuous training brings to the enterprise. Training of the workforce in new procedures, process practices, technical tools and techniques, languages, interpersonal skills, and the CE's mode of operation all multiply the value the employee brings to the organization.

Most organizations either don't invest seriously in training; or, at the slightest hint of slowing revenues, they are quick to pull the plug on the training budget. This is a big mistake.

The CE is very aware of the value of continued training, and they pursue it on multiple fronts. They look to spend their training budget very judiciously; and, they will use outside training classes, bring trainers into the company, and conduct their own training using company expertise.

The CE wants a workforce that is prepared to carry out their job functions, while being as versatile as possible in preparation for assisting with, other functions, as needed. The higher the expertise level of the workforce, the greater their confidence and ability to perform. The greater the flexibility of the workforce, the higher the productivity level of the organization.

With a more confident, productive and flexible workforce, the higher the return-on-investment will be to the organization for its training efforts and expenditure.

Factor # 3: Mentoring

I have had several mentors in my career, but none was more effective than when I worked for a heavy-duty truck manufacturing company in the Northwest. A new General Manager joined our team as the new Plant Manager. He was close to retirement and was back in the U.S. after having managed our operations in Australia.

He pulled the management team together by informing us that the best way for us to work together and understand each other's daily challenges was to live in each other's "shoes" for one month. Therefore, we set up a rotation cycle, where, every month, each top department manager, would move into another department manager's position.

On a Monday morning, I reported to Engineering as the Engineering Manager, remaining in that position for one month, before moving to the next assignment, as, perhaps, the Purchasing or Assembly Manager.

It took several months to make the full cycle. Did we all benefit from the experience? I know I certainly did. Did it require strong personnel under the rotating positions? Yes. Did they continue the program after our cycle? I believe so.

I heard there had been the implementation of more, smaller groups of mentoring within the entire organization, all because of one man's vision, I will never forget him or learning firsthand the benefits of mentoring. Mentoring is one-on-one, real-time and on-the-job. Consequently, I believe that mentoring is the most effective means of training.

Factor #4: Training Some More

When you believe everyone has been trained and mentored, train each one again. As the years go by, the life cycle of technologies, techniques and practices is becoming shorter and shorter. New opportunities to perform new tasks, work with new materials, integrate new systems, interact with new teams and streamline operations, are ever-present in today's work environments. Continuous training, especially as an on-the-job or an employee rotation program, should be viewed as critical to the organization's effectiveness and efficiency, just as its commitment to continuous improvement is to its operational processes.

Factor #5: Evaluating Results

All aspects of the Collaborative Enterprise are based on evaluating results, whether operating activities or, in this case, performance of the workforce.

Leading, teaching, and mentoring are not guarantees that the workforce automatically will be engaged with the CE operating environment. You must stay "in tune" as to "how" things are being done by the workforce. Evaluate the workforce. On-the-job training and mentoring provide real-time, immediate results and those are possible to evaluate.

On the other hand, for positions where such techniques are not practical, a formal evaluation process is needed. Each member of the workforce, management and workers alike, deserves to know what is expected of him/her, how each is doing, and what is needed for personal improvement. Most organizations have a formal, performance goal-setting and review process conducted annually as a minimum.

The CE works on a **continuous feedback strategy** but also provides for a quarterly, formal, written review process. It is important to recognize that the CE *does not wait* until the formal performance review process to provide the employee with feedback. It is instantaneous and in real time. Employees who perform above expectation levels are acknowledged for their efforts through incentive or recognition programs. For employees not performing satisfactorily, a performance-improvement process is initiated and documents, actions, and resolutions required for the employee to return to a satisfactory performance level are recorded.

Establishing performance goals that support the evolution of the CE's principles and evaluating the workforce's performance to those goals will help reinforce the importance of the organization's commitment to becoming a Collaborative Enterprise.

Factor #6: Using Self-Directed Teams

Empowering the workforce to make decisions and complete complex tasks as cross-functional teams creates an elevated level of trust between the leadership and workforce.

Teams and team leaders are hand-picked to perform specific tasks. The leadership and the team meet to review the requirements or purpose and to discuss and collaborate on desired results. This is the "delegate and coach" aspect of the CE that is not found in the traditional organization.

If there are resource constraints, e.g., budget dollars, equipment capacities, labor limitations, or time-frame, these are discussed, in advance, with the team.

Once the team is briefed on the activity, the team appoints a team leader from their group and proceeds with the activity or project. At that point, the team will apportion its workload, events, activities and desired results to each team member. The team leader will work within the team to evaluate progress, resolve issues, report status and help to manage available resources.

Leadership turns the activity over to the self-directed team because they know that the team has the skill, direction and target resolution for the project or activity. Leadership is now letting the self-directed team determine the best approach to achieve the results within the overall constraints provided at the chartering stage.

The self-directed team treats each member with the same level of respect and authority. They all participate in discussions, provide feedback and assist each other, with a clear goal of completing the activity as planned.

The self-directed team is just that, a team. Not a group of individuals, but a group of team members who are more concerned with the results of their team for the good of the organization than they are with their own, personal gain. As the self-directed team approach promotes a greater level of team spirit within the organization, the leadership will see tangible evidence of the workforce becoming more engaged with the CE's principles.

Let's review the 32 traits of an effective team:

<u>Ten attributes of an effective team leader:</u>

- Creates a compelling mission for the team.

- Knows the priorities: 1. team mission, 2. team, 3. individual members and 4. himself/herself.

- Communicates concisely, clearly and openly. Communication occurs when both sides understand what the other is trying to convey—until then, there is just talking.

- Encourages feedback.

- Supports and encourages diversity.

- Supports members by mentoring and coaching.

- Delegates authority and accountability.

- Selects members for their skills and desire to participate.

- Promotes continuous improvement.

- Fosters a positive, team culture.

Seven qualities of an effective team member:

- Exhibits strong discipline skills.

- Has good communication skills.

- Is a proponent of working in teams.

- Enjoys collaboration with other members.

- Is self-motivated.

- Demonstrates a strong work ethic.

- Performs as self-directed within team roles and responsibilities.

Fifteen characteristics of an effective team:

- Shows clear purpose.

- Exhibits on-going supportive leadership, i.e., coaching/mentoring.

- Enables processes and structures.

- Functions as a supportive organization.

- Members possess the necessary skills.

- Displays commitment and trust of members.

- Defines clear roles and responsibilities.

- Believes in clear team ground rules and protocols.

- Employs open communication.

- Demonstrates performance goals and accountability.

- Uses adequate resources.

- Possesses support-group diversity.

- Comprises members who are us-directed.

- Functions as a self-directed group.

- Is driven continuously to improve.

Factor #7-Leading by Example

To engage the workforce in the evolutionary process of becoming a Collaborative Enterprise, the leadership at the highest level **must** lead by example. There is no room for "Do *as I say, not as I do*".

With the leadership's commitment to a change in operation comes the same dedication to a change in role for them. They are committing, to the entire organization to do away with the "demand and control" methodology and the welcoming of the "delegation and coaching" approach.

Leaders in the CE spend their time strategizing, interacting with their stakeholders and monitoring the results of the operations.

They focus on the positives and compensate for the negatives. They keep the organization focused on the long-term targets, not letting daily challenges distract the team from maintaining their forward momentum. They roll up their sleeves and pitch in when it is needed, showing the workforce they care more about the longevity of the organization than their positions within the organization.

All too often, I hear leaders use the word "respect" as though it is a perk that accompanies their title. Anytime a leader *demands* respect, a big, red flag should be raised. It should bear in big, white letters, the initials "NLH", for "No Leader Here". Leaders earn respect; they don't acquire it with their title, position or demands.

My years in the military taught me the big difference that exists between leadership and authority.

While serving in Viet Nam on active duty, I learned very quickly, to whom I wanted to entrust my life. It certainly was not the young 1st or 2nd Lieutenants who just arrived in the country a few days earlier. No, it was the First Sergeant or Sergeant Major, non-commissioned officers who had had several combat campaigns and missions under their belts. I did my job as best I could, while staying as close to them as possible.

If you want quick examples of true leaders, look no further than the armed forces, your local police, firefighters and other first-responder organizations. There may be politics in each of these organizational structures, but they are the breeding grounds for true leaders.

Politicians and executives do not have their or others' lives on the line the way these service groups do. Most politicians and executives are out for themselves, first, and for others later.

Ask yourself, "Why do executives have to negotiate elaborate contracts with the Board of Directors before accepting their position? Who are they protecting?" True leaders look at the situation and say, "Follow me." Then, they are the first to move. "Empty-suits", a description for those who want to be considered leaders but lack the talent, shout orders from a distance, ensuring that they are out of harm's way.

CEs employ true leaders who really believe that the organization does come first. The driving force for this "true" leader is not a compensation package, designed to make him/her wealthy for life. No, these leaders have a goal of helping the company to grow and mature under their direction, enabling the next leader to continue the quest to be "better" than the last. Under this leadership style, the workforce will become quickly engaged.

Key Pieces:

- The workforce is the organization's asset and key stakeholder.

- There are seven ways to engage the workforce:

  - *Hiring* the right personnel to fit the culture.

  - *Training* the workforce continually to increase skills and flexibility.

  - *Mentoring* is the most effective way to train and influence performance.

  - *Training more* and more - producing the results of a more productive workforce.

  - *Evaluating results* of the workforce provides both the personnel and the organization feedback on performance.

  - *Utilizing self-directed teams* is key to improving communication, leadership stratification and loyalty.

  - *Leading by example* is advice for the leadership. Show the workforce how they are to perform and interact. Leaders are team members.

Create an Ecosystem

As we have mentioned in earlier chapters, the Collaborative Enterprise functions internally as an "Ecosystem." We have used this term to accentuate the importance of functional integration throughout the organization. The importance of the interdependence that each function has on one another to keep the organization in balance is critical to the success of the CE. Since there are not many manuals available to show how to create an ecosystem, let's explore a few ways to move in that direction. Again, this is a part of the evolution toward creating a Collaborative Enterprise.

Tear down the walls. For years, the open-office concept has been accepted as a way to increase communication and promote teamwork within the workplace. The CE's ecosystem promotes interaction across functions and by removing any obstacle giving the appearance of or actually impeding the ability for functions to interact more effectively.

The impediments to which I am referring are physical. There will always be a need for privacy; but, that can be handled with adequate meeting space, "war rooms", team spaces, very low-level partitioning, interior design, use of vegetation, and adequate "white noise" throughout the work area.

In Japan, there are examples of major corporations where the Chief Executive Officer and his key lieutenants all occupy the same office space. They do this to ensure that they are working together, to have immediate real-time open communication, and, I suspect, (I have not confirmed this) to encourage their loyalty.

"One for all and all for one." No, I am not talking about the Three Musketeers. I am describing the inter-workings of the operating mechanism of an ecosystem; the Collaborative Enterprise ecosystem thrives on the "oneness" of the organization. There are skill and functional separations, but they are in activities that do not require departmental integration.

A controller does not need a customer care expert to be involved with posting accounts payable or doing payroll, but such skills may be necessary when processing accounts receivable. That same controller will need involvement from the purchasing group when it comes to vendor/supplier management and payment issues. Since those vendor/suppliers are part of the CE's stakeholder group, there must be a coordinated effort to interact with these stakeholders in the most effective manner, by maintaining their partnership-type relationship. Having input from cross-functional groups that have dealings with the vendor/supplier in question may provide the controller invaluable information needed to bring an issue quickly and smoothly to closure.

A key point is that the other groups are committed to helping the controller, without prompting or demands. There are those who attempt to bring about the misfortunes of others to elevate their position. These are *saboteurs* and they will surface quickly within the CE work environment.

The CE is comprised of "helpers" not *saboteurs*. You are more likely to find fellow-workers reaching out to co-workers to help in any way that will improve the co-workers' positions. Ecosystems are self-balancing. When a problem arises in one area, in order to restore that balance, the other areas come to their aid.

Politics is for politicians. Unfortunately, politics can exist within any organization. There are those who try to position themselves for the accumulation of power and to position themselves to increase their personal gain. These individuals become identifiable more quickly within a CE than in traditional organizations.

During the evolution of the CE, there will be many struggles to root out these detrimental personality types — especially within the leadership — from the organization. They position themselves to receive the greatest amount of positive exposure from anyone they feel can provide them with favors, e.g., promotions, bonuses, raises, comp-time, etc., with the least amount of risk and accountability.

Again, these individuals are "empty-suits". Empty-suits are identified by their maneuverability *away* from doing work and taking risk. They want responsibility *without* accountability. They are more concerned about being "politically correct" in what they do and say, than the results they achieve. These personnel are not the team players who will go out of their way to help others for the good of the organization.

Such politicians are found at all levels of the organization. They are CEOs, Board of Director chairpersons, vice-presidents and directors, shop stewards, supervisors and individual workers. The good news is that if the company is truly committed to the CE's principles, as the workforce becomes more engaged in the CE evolution process, these personnel will exit the enterprise.

Teams are the catalyst. The existence of self-directed, cross-functional teams is one of the key indicators that the organization or company is evolving into a Collaborative Enterprise.

I have identified the need for the removal of physical separation where possible. The same is true within the operating process of the company. Very few operating activities *should* exist in isolation. For example, product development, research, problem resolution, system development/integration, customer service, manufacturing, finance, marketing/sales, etc. should all be able to benefit from synergy. Notice I said "should", but we know that in the traditional organization, those functional separations do exist and are highly protected.

Teams, working on common goals, fuel the multiplier effect for any company. Fresh ideas, multiple thoughts, cross-functional experiences, enhanced learning by personal interaction, and increased workforce flexibility are just some of the benefits of working in cross-functional teams.

Add "self-direction" that comes from the delegation portion of the CE's principles, and the team blossoms from the independence and trust they receive from leadership and the organization as a whole. Bringing together hand-picked individuals to participate in cross-functional teams to work for the common good of the enterprise is the very essence of the term "collaboration".

The corporate ecosystem will maintain a greater sense of balance if there is an integration of functionality throughout the enterprise. By addressing these challenges with a cohesive team approach to its solutions — albeit the ecosystem, it will be more responsive to the challenges it frequently endures.

Organizational sustainability. "Sustainability" can be defined as the ability of an ecosystem to maintain ecological processes, functions, bio-diversity and productivity into the future" (Wikipedia); or, simply put, the organization will endure into the future. Organizational sustainability as a priority for the leadership is a key differentiator between the Collaborative Enterprise and the traditional organization.

The key decision-makers are working to develop, perfect, test, implement and adjust the strategies, tactics and processes that make the company "better." Again, the goal is not to reach for perfection, just something better. The engaged workforce has the same mantra; they are continually working to change the operating characteristics of the organization to make it better than it was yesterday and to keep it in a position to perform even better in the future. They see no end to the organization's existence. Like any ecosystem, it has developed the attitude, work ethic, talent and processes to keep it operating in balance well into the future.

Key Pieces:

- Developing an ecosystem demonstrates an understanding of the value of functional interdependence.

- Ways to create an ecosystem in your organization:

    - *Tear down the physical and political walls,* to increase communication and cooperation.

    - *Engender a one-for-all-and-all-for-one attitude* to promote team work and cooperation between functions.

    - *Keep the politics out of the culture,* even if it means losing personnel once thought to be indispensable.

    - *Politics are for politicians.*

    - *Produce the most effective change.* Self-directed, cross-functional *teams are the catalyst.*

    - *Strive for organizational sustainability.* This means that the culture endeavors to conduct its high standard of performance forever. Everyone is always working to be better at what he/she does.

Engage the Other Stakeholders

The stakeholders, who are very important to the Collaborative Enterprise, are the workforce, customers, owners, suppliers/ vendors, the community, governmental organizations, and, even competitors. All these stakeholders must be engaged, at some level, to assist the CE to move forward with its agenda of providing high-quality products to the market faster and at lower price points than the competition — while maintaining sustainable profits.

The stakeholders are viewed as key components to the CE's ability to perform to its collective expectations. The CE views its relationship with the stakeholder as a "partnership." Even its competitors are viewed as stakeholders. The CE operates under an understanding that, at a certain level, it must establish a conditional partnership with its competitors.

Note: we have already discussed the importance of and methods of engaging the workforce. Therefore, let us now focus on possible ways to engage the remaining stakeholders.

Customers. You engage your customers by "listening" to them, having a forum where you can interact with them by sharing ideas; soliciting opinions; and, most importantly, finding out what they want.

Product delivery has changed significantly over the past two decades, and those companies that are in tune with their customers are delivering product on demand, or employing the "pull" strategy. The customer orders the features, colors, etc., desired and the product arrives within days.

Dell Computer and others have been recognized as leaders in this area. Amazon.com is not recognized as a book reseller, as once thought. It is a real-time distribution company. You select what you want, pay for it, and in two days, it is delivered by Fedx, UPS, or USPS.

The traditional "push" method of product delivery is most recognized as the "Henry Ford approach," where the company professes to know what is best for the customer and delivers that product in the colors, features and price points they "assume" the customer wants.

In addition to closing the quality gap, the foreign auto manufacturers were first to allow the customer to select the color, features and configurations, and, receive the product within weeks. That "pull" approach rewarded these manufacturers with a significant market share in the automotive industry, and the U.S. manufacturers are still struggling to recover their competitive foothold.

The CE knows that it must be *continually* in touch with as large a segment of its customer base as possible. It knows that it must listen to their needs, wants and desires, and capitalize on this information to meet or exceed the customers' expectations. It uses focus groups, surveys, community and industry events, the Internet, and other means to *gather* customer information.

Traditional organizations spend their time, dollars and efforts *advertising* their thoughts to their customers, but they do very little listening. The key listening post of the traditional organization, often too deaf to the pearls of wisdom of the customer, is the traditional sales person. Their common mistake is in their compartmentalized vision of their goals. They are set up to "sell new product" and leave the customer research to the marketing department and others.

The CE is clever. It uses its own employees as their first input group. They invest their resources in their customers, knowing that the returns they will receive are not only revenues, but, even more importantly to the CE, "loyal customers" who trust their products and services. These consumers will repeat the buying experience because of the connected relationship established with the CE as a provider of products and services desired.

The customers are true stakeholders in the eyes of the Collaborative Enterprise and and they see the results of their dialog developing into products and services that the customers want to buy.

Owners. Owners are probably the most obvious "stakeholder" found on the list. After all, they own the company. If the company does well, they may be financially rewarded. If the company fails, they lose their investment.

There are active and passive owners. The size and structure of the enterprise, as well as the personality and confidence of the Chief Executive Officer, will determine the owners' level of participation in the activities of the organization.

In the traditional sense, the pecking order for responsibility starts with the owners. They are responsible for appointing a Board of Directors, often structured to include an owner majority, which provides oversight to the leadership of the enterprise, usually the Chief Executive Officer (CEO).

The CEO has responsibilities for oversight for the rest of the leadership and day-to-day operations of the company.

An organization may not have a Board of Directors or a CEO. The owner/operator of a small or mid-size, privately-held organization still has the same responsibilities and accountabilities to his/her company. The commitment to create a Collaborative Enterprise must be endorsed by the ownership, even if it is a single owner/operator. The ownership's understanding of the evolutionary process the company will undergo and how the leadership and workforce will deal with issues encountered is extremely important to the success of the company.

The management leadership must develop the ownership's trust by finding ways to communicate frequently at levels that keep the owners engaged in the organization's progress, without opening an avenue for being micro-managed.

A CE's owner is engaged through open, frequent and quality two-way communication. The Collaborative Enterprise CEO is not a "may-I" manager. The owners and Board of Directors *should not*, and usually are not involved in the day-to-day operations within the CE, or any organization, for that matter.

Suppliers/Vendors. Similarly to the owners, the suppliers/vendors clearly *should be* identified as stakeholders to any organization.

This is not the case for most traditional organizations. For these organizations, suppliers/vendors are viewed as necessary *evils*. They are looked at with distain and are often the brunt of mistreating buyers because they know that the supplier/vendor needs their business to sustain itself.

I presented at a conference where many of the attendees were suppliers/vendors to the airline manufacturing industry. My discussions with them spanned several topics, one being the area of "supply-chain management." Several supplier/vendors were extremely frustrated with their customers. Having implemented the "required" information systems and functionality to support their supply-chain management program mandate, these supplier/vendors were still receiving orders at the last minute. They were frequently surprised by engineering changes, continually being pounded on price and required to carry additional inventory, at no cost to their customers.

The Collaborative Enterprise takes a different view of these stakeholders. It sees the stakeholders as partners. The CE knows that it cannot produce the products and services wanted by its customers without a trusted, reliable and price-competitive supplier/vendor network behind it. The CE establishes a rapport with the suppliers/vendors that aligns both entities' business strategies, tactics and execution methods.

The level of trust and degree of involvement between the CE and its supplier/vendors comes after a thorough vetting process and a tested relationship; it does not happen overnight. The CE will go as far as to set up exclusive arrangements with key supplier/vendors requiring joint business planning and tactical exercises to insure that both companies are involved in the details of contributing to each other's success.

The Collaborative Enterprise knows that a supplier/vendor, who is treated with respect and honesty, is one that eventually can be trusted to perform and remain at its side along the path of operating sustainability. This level of engagement with suppliers and vendors is an area where, in a very positive way, the CE truly stands out as being unique.

Community. Most professionals don't recognize community, governments and competitors as stakeholders, but the Collaborative Enterprise does.

Why the community? First, where do the leadership and workforce at the CE come from or where do they reside? The community. This same community in which the CE operates, both domestically and internationally, depending on the locations of the CE's facilities, provides a great deal of the resources needed by the organization.

The infrastructure, marketplace, recreation, education, healthcare, transportation, etc. are all services that the community provides to the organizations that exist within its boundaries. In turn, the community has needs that the organization can support.

There may be resource shortages in areas within the community that the Collaborative Enterprise will enter into arrangements to support.

There are worthy charities and support organizations that need financial assistance, volunteers and access to special services, equipment and talent. The CE knows that when it reaches out to support this stakeholder, called "community," it is gaining the respect and trust of those who work around and within the organization, purchasing their products and services.

Knowing that the community and CE must co-exist in a positive manner is why the Collaborative Enterprise is so committed to engaging the community as a partner in its operation.

Governments. Yes, governments, whether local, state or federal, are included on the list of stakeholders for the Collaborative Enterprise. Governments are not usually viewed favorably by an enterprise. They are the tax collectors, regulating and bureaucratic organizations that seem to cause problems, not solve them. Depending on your perspective, all those things may be true.

Government is not going away any time soon, and the Collaborative Enterprise knows that. If the CE operates under one or more regulatory agencies, then it is extremely involved, either directly with the agencies or through special lobbyists, interest groups and industry associations.

The CE knows that it is better to participate as an "influencer" than to be "influenced." A single organization may not be able to directly influence a local, state or federal agency; but, the involvement with these entities, in a positive and constructive way, can only improve the prospects for positive results.

Yes, the CE must pay taxes, like any other organization. The CE has examined the overall entitlements and assessments associated with its locations, products and services produced, the location of its customers and the industry in which it operates. It has made a conscious decision to be where it is. Its people understand the impacts that governments have on their strategies, and they, willingly, engage these governing bodies as stakeholders.

Competitors. How can a competitor be a stakeholder? Good question! If you think of a stakeholder as someone who has something to either gain or lose from the actions of another organization or person, you can probably begin to see a connection. Marketing professionals often define market efficiency by the level of competition, and if there is no competition, there cannot be an efficient market.

The Collaborative Enterprise looks at competitors in a slightly different light than the traditional organization. Competitors are not people you are out to destroy or cause harm to. The CE looks at the competitors in their industry much like professional level athletic competitors. When watching any sport, such as tennis, baseball, football, soccer, swimming, track, snowboarding, etc., you see a tremendous amount of competition. Yet, after the match, game, or event, an equal amount of respect for the competitors exists.

Professional athletes will tell you that the greater the competition, the higher level of performance they generate. It brings out the best in them, thus producing greater results. As a result of such competition, they are more eager to train and participate. The CE looks at its competitors in much the same way. They want to surpass the competition in their marketplace; because, they planned, strategized, executed and produced more than the competition, not because they were able to undercut their products, spread rumors about their services or leadership, or speak of them in a negative way to potential buyers. The CE will reach out to its competitors if they suffer catastrophic situations causing irrefutable harm. If a key piece of equipment fails and parts are not readily available, a CE may loan the competitor a part. If the competitor ends up with costly excess inventory, the CE may negotiate its purchase.

The CE believes competition is important to their industry, giving it something to strive for, to be the best they can be.

The CE will use industry and association activities to develop rapport with its competitors. It will work together on initiatives possibly threatening their industry or specific markets.

The Collaborative Enterprise knows that, by engaging their completion as a stakeholder, a merger or acquisition opportunity may present itself in the future. To paraphrase a famous saying, "Keep your friends close and your competitors closer."

Key Pieces:

- Recognize the total number of stakeholders who have an impact on the success of the organization.

- *Customers*- Know what is most important to the customers and have them involved in the design, deployment and support of products and services.

- *Owners*- Communication and relationship-building are management/leadership responsibilities.

- *Suppliers/Vendors*- A partnership relationship will produce greater efficiencies, lower costs and greater flexibility. Increase communication, planning and strategies with qualified suppliers/vendors.

- *Community*- A source of customers, workforce, vendor/suppliers and facility support services. Providing resources in support of community charities, events and activities all develop a positive relationship with the community.

- *Governments*- Local, state and federal institutions have an impact on the organization and that positive interaction and cooperation will yield benefits over the long-term.

- *Competitors*- Competition creates markets and the goal is not to crush the competition but to beat them in the marketplace. Helping them, when necessary, and cooperating in association and industry events will create a cordial relationship.

Establish Real-time Information

There is a distinct difference between *data* and *information*. *Data* are facts and content which, alone, appear meaningless and useless. When data are filtered, processed, translated or presented in an organized manner, they become more useful and are referred to as *Information*.

Some say you cannot have enough data. The quantity of data is of no consequence to the Collaborative Enterprise, which recognizes that it is the information needed that is most important. It massages, interprets and filters a variety of data sources into useful value-based information.

Value-based information is different from ordinary information. *Value-based* implies that an additional level of distillation of the information sources into a more critical set of facts and inputs exists. These are more useful to the organization and its decision-making processes.

For example, useful, ordinary information to a battery manufacturer would be having knowledge of how many cars the manufacturer is going to produce. Value-based information further defines the manufacturer's plans into the number of 12-volt batteries of a certain size (12" x 6" x 8") that the auto manufacturer has engineered into its new models. The CE continually pursues the "value based" information, not just data.

Information Integrity. You are probably familiar with the saying "garbage in, garbage out." This phrase has been around for several decades, and is as relevant today as it was when first introduced within the information technology industry.

If the source of the information is tainted by errors in collection, interpretation and organization, it contributes to erroneous information everywhere that this source is used. Therefore, the accuracy of information sources is tied to the value the information brings to the up-stream use of that information.

For instance, if a company omits certain material expenses in its calculation for cost of goods sold (COGS), then COGS, overstates the gross profits. If the company includes those material costs as operating expenses, then they are overstating those expenses and polluting all analyses of operating expenses, including profit ratios and possible expense-reduction measures.

The CE is highly focused on the collection and manipulation of accurate and value-based information; and, before using it in any critical analysis, knows the information sources must be tested, verified and justified.

Information Timeliness. Information integrity referred to the accuracy of the source. However, information timeliness refers to the freshness of the information. Most traditional organizations manage their performance by using their financial statements to conduct trend analysis. As a few examples, they check profitability, expense tracking, sales and revenue performance.

What is wrong with this approach? In this case, the information being used to manage the organization is at least 30-45 days old. I call this practice "managing from the rear-view mirror approach." There is nothing wrong with using old information for making year-over-year comparisons. However, traditional accounting and financial practices use this less-timely information for supporting the day-to-day operating management of the enterprise.

On the other hand, the CE believes in managing its organization by "looking through the windshield, not the rear-view mirror." That is why availability of real-time, value-based information is so critical to the CE's ability to be more effective and efficient than its competition.

The CE has processes and technology that provide this value-based information to the appropriate decision-makers as close to real-time as possible. There are real-time *scorecard* or *dashboard* systems that provide graphical or numerical representations of data that is rapidly processed. Many of these systems are appended to an organization's financial system, before being displayed. Much of the information must be collected and filterd in the primary system (financial or others) before it can be displayed by a scorecard or dashboard application. Real-time display systems work very well for those companies looking to track financial and operating changes and trends as events happen. The CE has processes which also use these scorecard or dashboard systems, but it has technologies and processes that are looking at information that has not yet been collected through their financial, purchasing, sales or marketing operating systems. This information is related to industries, products, politics, technology, and innovation and is indirectly relevant to the CE mission and overall operations.

Information Overload. I recently read an article that claimed that the more information you can collect, the better your decisions. Depending on the context of such a statement, I would agree; but, this article was proposing that the quantity of information, itself, will encourage better decision-making. I would amend this statement a little by saying that the more *value-based* information you have, the better chance you have of making better decisions.

The CE qualifies the information elements it needs to contribute to its decision-making processes. Furthermore, where the information is used up-stream of the decision-making process, it establishes processes that ensure the integrity and timeliness of that data. This is how the CE nurtures its value-based information.

If your organization relies on collecting all the "data" it can, while trying to "slice-and-dice" it in any number of ways, chances are your result will be information overload. How do you know if you are in *overload?* My test is to evaluate if, after all the slicing-and-dicing, the information actually has been used in the decision-making process.

When I was managing information technology functions, I would often halt the distribution of reports which I felt were not being used. I then waited to see how long it would take to receive a complaint. Most often, this action resulted in the suspension of such reports, because they were no longer being used and had not been missed.

Collecting, organizing, interpreting and *using* the most current information will help prevent information-overload.

Forward-looking Performance Tracking. Making business decisions by looking through the windshield rather than the rear-view mirror is what we call "forward-looking".

As mentioned earlier, far too many enterprises determine their performance by using their financial statements to establish metrics and tracking targets. These indicators are fine when tracking historical trends and comparing year-over-year statistics, but they are almost useless within a flexible company for assisting in making day-to-day operating decisions.

This is because the data are seldom released for review by the accounting professionals until they know the numbers will withstand an audit. The results, at best, are a minimum of 15-30 days after the close of the period (month, quarter, year, etc.). That delay means that decisions you wanted to make in the beginning of a month will not be supported by that month's relevant data for another 45 to 60 days.

Instead of being bound to delayed information, the Collaborative Enterprise spends a great deal of time and effort in evaluating data points within the company, their industry and the global economy at-large, while looking for events, conditions, trends and relationships that may yield a glimpse of the impact on its future business — both near and long-term.

Some examples that might be used for evaluation could be: seats purchased by a certain segment of traveler for an airline, emerging regulatory requirements or fuel-efficiency standards for over-the-road hauling limitations to a truck manufacturer, anticipated levels of international travel to various transporters (air, land and sea) and tour companies, or the weather forecast for the next decade to those that select food, feed or energy crops for their fields. There is seldom a single factor that a company will track to assist in its decision-making. The more metrics and the tighter the relationship between them, the more useful the information will be to the decision-makers. No matter if the company is tracking one or 100 metrics, the key is that they are based on accurate, current or future indicators being utilized — not those of the past. Finding these forward-looking data points and filtering them into useful information is very time-consuming and can be expensive; but, once the correlation is found, the benefits are significant.

Enabling Technologies. Be thankful that the information-storage industry has kept *ahead* of the information-generation and storage demands of the world. You can now purchase Terabytes of storage for the same price megabytes cost just 24 months ago.

The computing technology life cycle and a variety of distribution methods continue to open the door of opportunity to every enterprise, regardless of size or location, to access relevant and critical information.

At one time, the Internet was used as the supreme means to disseminate and review a vast oasis of information. In a very short period of time, it was transformed into an efficient and relatively effective data-collection device. Now, not only can the data be viewed, analyzed, evaluated, collected and filtered in real-time with a couple clicks of a mouse, but it can also be translated, converted to text or voice, transformed from graphic images to video and distributed in unlimited directions.

As amazing as technologies are, those organizations on the evolutionary road to becoming a CE know that these are means to an end. The CE knows that these technologies do not always come with fraud-proof analyzers to determine which data or information is accurate or being interpreted accurately.

The CE knows that billions of dollars are spent annually on implementations of Customer Relationship Management (CRM) and Enterprise Resource Planning (ERP) systems and the returns are never realized. Why? The company's culture, leadership, focus and the required resources were not in place to utilize these valuable tools. These companies made a decision to implement such systems, because the company needed a technology to compete; but, the true returns were never calculated with the company's environmental factors taken into consideration.

Billions of dollars will be spent in reworking the implementation, trying to integrate the technologies with legacy or outdated systems and infrastructure, and hiring key personnel to lead the project to a satisfactory conclusion. A satisfactory conclusion does not mean the originally-planned conclusion, but just a condition of "getting it up and running."

Technology by itself will not transform any enterprise into a sustainable organization. It is the artful application of that technology that will make the difference. When a company knows its business and where technology will help more effectively gain the desired results, that company has a greater chance for success.

Business Intelligence. Having the correct information available at the time decisions must be made is the overall objective of "business intelligence." That information may be about a competitor and its products, the markets you supply or the industry in which you participate. Such information may concern international socio-economic issues which will have a bearing on where the next facility is constructed, what level of outsourcing or partnering should be pursued, or the forecasts on currency valuations.

There are thousands of decisions an organization must make daily, and the greater the amount of "intelligence" it has about its overall business objectives, the less risk there is for failure. However, there are no guarantees that the information you gather will produce the 100% results you hope for. If your organization realizes the value of business intelligence and has a process for identifying, gathering, and analyzing that information to be used in a timely manner, then the opportunity for your organization to achieve positive results is greater than if you had done less.

Key Pieces:

- Data is a collection of facts and information. Filtered and organized data creates value.

- *Information integrity-* Knowing the source of the information and its accuracy is key to the value of the decisions made based on that information.

- *Information timeliness-* Real-time information is very valuable to immediate decision making and ties together the CE operation.

- *Information overload-* Too much data is distracting and must be qualified into value-based information.

- *Forward-looking Performance tracking-* Information that comes from external sources that provides *future* impacts, both positive and negative. Looking through the windshield instead of the rear-view mirror.

- *Enabling technologies-* Storage technologies and distribution techniques such as the Internet allow organizations of all sizes, to collect, filter, test and forward high volumes of information that improve their decision-making capabilities.

- *Business intelligence-* Taking the value-based information and using it to make value-based decisions about one's industry, markets, competitors and operating strategies.

Practice Continuous Improvement

Change is threatening to most of us. Everyone has comfort zones, at work and at home; and, because these zones are *comfortable*, we find it hard to escape them.

I once saw a poster that said, "A status quo operation produces status quo results." Most companies want to operate in the status quo, while still wanting to increase innovation and growth. It seems to be the fear of taking risks that causes organizations to settle into the status quo and become content with their mediocre results. Unfortunately, that settling is unfair to the stakeholders at every level.

I don't propose that every organization should be driven to become the next Microsoft, GE, or Wal-Mart. However, I would suggest that, regardless of the size or type of organization you have, you should challenge yourself and your organization to strive to be better tomorrow than it is today.

Voltaire said, "Perfect is the enemy of the good." For my purposes, I have rephrased this quotation as, "Best is the enemy of better." For years, I have used this observation when explaining that there is lost benefit when trying to make something the best it can be before the project, product, solution, graphic, article, etc. has been launched.

Here is an example: I don't support premature offerings when they are not ready for "prime time." However, if I can proceed with a "better" process or product while further developing additional features or functions, then I receive the benefits of the difference between the two launch dates.

Continuous improvement is a cornerstone for the Collaborative Enterprise and, within most organizations, it should be an attribute *at all levels*. Continuous improvement has no ending point. The CE makes it a part of its corporate DNA. It transcends beyond each new CEO, product launch and acquisition.

Continuous improvement has many labels and most see it as a manufacturing phenomenon. In reality, it can and should be applied to all aspects of the enterprise.

Lean Management. There is a strong movement toward Lean Management practices in the manufacturing sector, especially the automotive and aerospace industries. This is thanks to the work of Toyota; to John Krafcik, the president and CEO of Hyundai, and co-authors of *The Machine That Changed the World*, James Womack, Daniel Jones and Daniel Roos.

In general, the principles of Lean Management are derived from the Japanese disciplines for removing waste, improving flow and eliminating errors.

The purpose of the rest of this chapter is to discuss the overall benefits of developing methods that work for each organization to improve what they do each and every day. Whether you implement a formal Lean Management discipline or other documented process-improvement techniques — or whether you adopt your own processes and techniques for identifying and reducing waste, improving processes and getting more done with fewer resources — the overall objective will be the same. You are striving to become a more effective and efficient company – you are Creating a Collaborative Enterprise-type company.

Effective vs. efficient. There is a clear difference between being *effective* and being *efficient*. Effectiveness demonstrates how well you are hitting your targets. Efficiency means how well you accomplish something with fewer resources, e.g., financial, personnel, raw material, machine time, total hours, etc.

Training. In my opinion, the most misunderstood activity and expenditure in an organization is that of training. Training has been discussed in detail in previous chapters. However, let us not underestimate the importance of having an engaged workforce, all working from the same tactical plan.

Military leaders don't hand out a strategic plan to their division leaders and say, "Use whatever methods you want; just win the battle." No, they have a very detailed, choreographed plan explaining everyone's role, objective and the methods to be deployed. If you want to convert a workforce from the *status quo to a status better us*, then you need to provide continuous and consistent training on what to look for, how to value the change, and how to change it.

If the organization is not experienced with process improvement, it would certainly benefit from an outside expert's assistance in developing the strategies for establishing a continuous, improvement-oriented work force.

Based on your strategies and basic guidelines, who will best develop this training? Your work force, of course. They already know many of the changes needed to take place, but they have not had a process in place to evaluate and implement them.

Here is a key point: *Continuous improvement is not a program; it is a company's cultural characteristic.* Programs, like projects, have a beginning and an end. In order to create a cultural change in the work force, the leadership of the company must continually train and mentor in the techniques and processes developed to identify, classify, and implement improvements in all aspects of the operation.

Work flow analysis. I had a client that was a telecommunications company. When asking a customer care representative why he documented his customer call the way he did, he responded, "Because that is the way we have always done it." Legacy manual *processes* are just as prevalent in organizations as are legacy information technology *systems* and for the same reason. *We are comfortable with them and we don't want to change.*

Several companies are now embarking on significant projects to conduct work-flow analysis of their processes, whether they are on the manufacturing floor or in the back room. These might include accounting, sales, marketing, customer care, purchasing, shipping, IT, etc.

Work-flow analysis can take many forms, but the basics are to identify each and every step in a process and evaluate what value that step contributes to the overall process. Your questions might include: Who uses the step? What are its inputs and outputs from and to other steps? Who is responsible for the step? What does the step cost in people, infrastructure, equipment, etc.? Are there similar steps used in other areas? These are just a sample of the types of questions to be asked during the analysis process.

It is very important to have cross-functional input to the analysis and it does not matter who, within the company, interacts with the "activity" or "step."

One visual technique that I often use is the production of a "process flow diagram." This is a simple flow chart, graphically reflecting all the steps in a process and illustrating how everything interacts with steps within other processes. It is a visual representation of the activities of a company and it is usually an eye-opener as to areas of a great deal of waste. Here are two examples of waste that nobody may realize is taking place until they look at a process diagram. (1) When data that is gathered, analyzed, translated, and reported on is no longer being used. (2) When multiple departments gather/handle the same information for the same purposes.

Corporations are expending resources to create process diagrams, not only to find duplication, dead ends, and to reduce waste, but to enhance their knowledge of their operations, helping to minimize the risk when a critical resource is lost. If the knowledge of how something works is only in the head of an employee, when that employee leaves the organization, the corporation has to absorb the cost of training a replacement. Work-flow analysis is an efficient way to identify waste, increase efficiency and increase knowledge across the organization as to what transpires within any given process.

Real-time testing. Many companies try to implement some form of *continuous improvement*, without achieving a lasting result. Why? Many reasons exist for false starts at continuous improvement, but one most commonly found is "analysis paralysis." In case we have not all heard the term, it means to delay implementing something — due to a prolonged period of analysis or study — to the point that the implementation is no longer beneficial.

On the other hand, continuous improvement refers to a set of tools, standards, techniques and processes that discourage rogue or freelance changes on the part of the workforce without regard to the implications to the company's operation or products.

Any company that has cultivated a "culture" of continuous improvement (remember, it is not a program) knows that it must move quickly, but intelligently, when it makes changes. That is why many companies utilize methods for real-time testing of their process-improvement tactics. Depending on the significance of the alteration or modification, these companies are able to develop a quick means to test their changes in a quasi-production environment and immediately evaluate the results. If the results are as expected, they have a seamless procedure for integrating the change into the operation.

These organizations are passionate about the continuous-improvement mindset. If they find a potential change that looks too large to attack immediately, they quickly divide the change into smaller events, addressing each subset as quickly as possible. Little analysis paralysis exists in these CE-type organizations. Testing in real-time provides a challenge and motivation to reduce risk and, hopefully, experience immediate gratification. Knowing that a better way to accomplish a task is "in process," truly inspires the corporation's workforce.

Cooperation. Many who write or speak about *collaboration* use the word *cooperation* as a synonym. I believe that is incorrect. To me, collaboration implies a greater involvement and commitment between parties. Do they need to cooperate? Yes. However, the various disciplines within an enterprise need to cooperate, as well, to effect continuous improvement! Some of the improvements may be contained within a specific discipline, department or function, but cooperation is still required.

Any time several people have to work together on resolving an issue, their interaction will determine the outcome of their efforts. The level of cooperation is increased when tasks must be resolved by two or more individuals from different disciplines, departments or functions.

Difficulty usually arises from different disciplines having different priorities. What may be important to me may not be as important to someone else. Yet, if all disciplines within an enterprise understand that they are there to make the organization better, there is less push-back as to priorities. I said, "Less." That does not mean there will be none, because no matter how committed the various organizational disciplines are to the overall good of the company, they will still have their "pet" projects.

It is vital that there be a process for evaluating the impact of change on ideas and the efforts to implement them. Furthermore, there needs to be a *referee* within the process evaluation activity to prioritize. Also, if the workforce is not engaged in the "attitude" of cooperation, it makes continuous improvement ineffective and sometimes, almost impossible.

Incentives. What motivates people? Thousands of books and articles have been written on this subject. Just check out Amazon.com and you'll find several books referring to ways of rewarding employees. Incentives are important to employees, regardless of how engaged they are in the Collaborative Enterprise approach to continuous improvement. There is nothing wrong with incentive or reward systems that are fair, unbiased and proportional to the benefits received by the company. Regrettably, most reward systems I have seen and participated in fell short of being very rewarding or fair. An employee making a suggestion for ways to save a company hundreds of thousands of dollars should not be rewarded with a $50 gift certificate to the Mall.

I believe the best approach is to reward the workforce on a percentage of actual (true) cost savings (or incremental revenues generated) for the first year. That is *cost savings, not cost* avoidance; there is a difference.

Cost avoidance means that an idea *may* save the company an expense that is *coming* but has not yet been realized. Therefore, those reward payments should be distributed not in lump sum, but on a quarterly basis, based on actual savings results. The incentive system must have a full accounting to the employee receiving the reward and to the organization. There should be no guess work, just facts as to cost savings (revenues) realized by the company for the period and the amount of the reward paid to the employee based on those savings.

Who should judge the actual awards of the programs? This should be done by a rotating board or committee composed of responsible individuals from within the workforce, along with management oversight. The reason for oversight by management is to insure a level playing field of fairness. Incentives are important to a continuous-improvement attitude within any organization, but they should not be the main driver for the workforce. The main objective for continuous improvement is seeing the organization grow, prosper and remain sustainable. Hopefully, an incentive payment would never be more important than having a place to work every day.

Never-ending. Continuous improvement is a never-ending process. Initially, it may feel like a program, because the organization is embarking on a new way of operating. However, if the company intends to become a Collaborative Enterprise, the priority of the evolutionary process must be to ingrain the continuous improvement mindset into the culture of the organization. With time, patience and a steady focus, the rewards and benefits are enormous, not just to the organization, but to the stakeholders, who are the contributors to the efforts to create and sustain the continuous improvement momentum. After the leadership and workforce are committed to Creating a Collaborative Enterprise, the evolution toward a continuous-improvement operating-environment will produce great rewards in the shortest period of time.

Key Pieces:

- Continuous improvement is an underlying attribute of the organization and is based on lean manufacturing techniques and tools.

- Focus is not on perfection but on being "forever better."

- *Training-* The workforce must endorse, understand and use the on-going, preferred techniques to improve all processes.

- *Workflow analysis* concerns breaking down a process into its smallest elements and removing those not adding value to the end result. Flowcharting makes it easier to evaluate users, benefactors and value.

- *Real-time testing-* Checking the results during the process flow, rather than waiting until its completion, increases efficiency. Using the Iterative Process Model endorses real-time testing.

- *Incentives-* If proportional and relative, incentives can increase engagement of the workforce, but they should be fair, un-biased and administered by a bi-partisan committee.

- *Never ending-* Continuous improvement is "continuous" because it is not a program but a mindset that is nurtured and valued by the organization as a key success factor.

Track Results

As with any organization, Traditional or Collaborative, there is a need to establish operating goals, objectives and to *track results*. Companies work hard on establishing strategic and tactical plans, but they often fall short on the discipline required for tracking their results against those plans. As stated in the chapter on forward-looking performance tracking, it is prudent to track results for the purpose of trending or making real-time decisions. Trending implies the use of *past* results to determine how the organization is performing against its own previous results or those of others — competitors, industries, etc.

As previously mentioned, there are software solutions called "scorecards" or "dashboards" that provide statistical and graphic representations of performance for areas in which the information is collected. The dashboards are most valuable when used for real-time decision-making, but they have uses when working on trending studies or analysis. Those enterprises not using tracking results or employing information to improve their decision-making capabilities are like the sailor on a ship without a rudder. How can the ship remain on course when you don't know where you are?

A saying used in reference to planning states, "If you don't know where you are going, any road will get you there." The same is true of an organization that does not track its results against its plans. Results are necessary to *correct its course,* if the organizational ship drifts off its planned route or the Captain decides to change direction to one more safely or efficiently able to reach the desired destination.

Operating metrics, (statistics) often found in the accounting or finance department in the form of financial ratios, such as balance sheet ratios, income statement ratios and asset management ratios, look backwards and are most effective for trending and evaluating past performance. The gathering of real-time information concerning operating results disseminated instantaneously, i.e., as timely as possible after filtering, is the best resource for making comparisons against goals and other desired performance results.

Key Pieces:

- Strategies, tactics, goals and objectives are of no value unless the results are tracked and measured against these plans.

- *Trend tracking* works well for looking back, and *performance-tracking* against external factors enhances real-time decision-making accuracy.

- Tracking and measuring results allows for course correction in a timely manner.

- Dashboard and scorecard software systems can assist in the dissemination of valuable, operating-performance information.

Operate an Inter-Collaborative Organization

As is evident at this point, the Collaborative Enterprise not only focuses on working jointly with its outside stakeholders, but it uses the same principles to operate collaboratively *internally.*

I have read articles which make statements that internal-collaboration stifles innovation and effectiveness, but I disagree. There are those who describe collaboration as *management by consensus.* In that case, I can see why they would believe collaboration is a time-waster and less productive. Our definition of *collaboration,* as explained in earlier chapters, is much more than *management by consensus.*

Note: If you believe, as I do, that two heads are better than one, you might enjoy reading *The Wisdom of Crowds* by James Surowiecki. This mindset also supports the benefits of collaboration.

The Collaborative Enterprise is unique, because it knows that its success is tied to the effectiveness of three things, which are their: *strategies, tactics,* and *execution.* Let's explore these three keys and see how they can be applied to any organization desiring to become a Collaborative Enterprise.

1. *Strategic thinking* does not come easily to most organizations. I have already defined a strategy as the *what, when or where* the company plans to use to move its mission forward. Strategic thinking is the prerequisite to conducting strategic planning. There are corporations that don't think strategically very well, yet they have a strategic plan. In reviewing that plan, you will find that it is a "tactical" plan, or the *how* things are going to be done.

Strategic thinking happens in many different ways, with no one way being superior to another. My preferred approach is creating "*what if*" scenarios, describing the *what, when* and *where*, and then, in a team environment, conducting a *Strength, Weakness, Opportunities and Threats* (SWOT) analysis or create a Pro and Con list for each of the scenarios. You may review several scenarios before selecting a strategy that best meets the mission of the company.

Strategic thinking works best when there is a diverse, cross-section of expertise and skill sets from within the organization. Notice that I did not mention what level these personnel should be. There should be a representation of those people, who have a clear understanding of the industry, markets, regulations, and the mission of the organization.

2. *Tactical approaches* are the *how* portion of achieving the company's mission. As with strategic thinking, the more participation of skilled and experienced personnel, the more effective the desired results will be.

There are always unintended consequences that materialize when tactics are not comprehensive. For best results, put the right personnel from all areas of the organization together in a room and list the possibilities for achieving the company's strategies in an apolitical manner.

Note: My reference to defining tactics in an *apolitical* manner is extremely important. I believe that office politics and power plays are the reason for most contamination or corruption of the planning activities within organizations.

Is personal gain the motivation for maintaining tactics in a political light? An organizational culture that is polluted with political correctness (PC) is only going through the motions. Its effectiveness will be delayed or curtailed completely due to the desire for personal gain by those influential enough to perpetuate the culture, e.g., the CEO, Chairman, Board of Directors, and C-level leadership team.

The interactive model discussed in prior chapters provides a methodology for creating effective tactics for achieving results. There is nothing magical about the interactive model. It provides a structure for communication and cooperation between different disciplines from within the company and a consolidated commitment to their results. The tactical approach endorsed by the company is the road map to be followed by the organization when execution begins.

3. *Execution initiatives* are those operating fronts which have the charter to complete tasks outlined by the tactical approach, by taking the tactical road map and following it. Execution initiatives are the application of resources to effect the results outlined by the tactical plan. This is the *doing* portion of the organizational planning process. The art of execution is best summarized by the steps found in good project management: establish the goal, break down the goal into smaller tasks, establish target deadlines, apply the resources to achieve each task, and monitor/adjust the efforts toward each task until it is satisfactorily completed.

For the success of an organization, *execution* requires the three C's of an effective operation: communication, cooperation and commitment.

1. Communication refers to making sure that the relevant inter/intra-company disciplines are aware of what actions are being taken, what the target results are and when the actions will be concluded.

2. *Cooperation* means that the people resources for an execution initiative are functioning as a team, working together in a coordinated effort. Remove the politics from the scene and most companies' workforces will work together for the good of the organization.

3. *Commitment* makes the assumption that all resources required to complete the tasks are made available when needed. The key resource is the company's *people*. Machines and systems don't seem to mind working together, if integrated properly. However, when you start requiring people to work together, a different situation arises. The level of *Commitment* to the execution initiative by the organization and the individuals working on that task is essential to its completion. If those working on the

task understand the importance to the company of their work, they are more likely to want to do a better job than those who are not convinced that their efforts will help the company. When summing up the beneficial impact on execution of the three Cs, you should begin to understand why the CE is so committed to the use of *self-directed, cross-functional teams*. These teams bring together different, inter-company disciplines involved in the execution of a task, as a team effort. The *team* structure promotes communication with the team members. It enhances cooperation between the team members and, in most cases, it fortifies the commitment of the members to their team and the mission of the team — to execute in a satisfactory manner.

If functioning independently, organizational departments don't permit the company to operate effectively. Functional disciplines must interact in order for the enterprise to operate efficiently and effectively. A Collaborative Enterprise would describe these internal disciplines that rely on each other as internal-stakeholders and components of the company's ecosystem. Every organization should realize that they have internal-stakeholders and promote increasing the level of communication, cooperation and commitment on the part of these internal-stakeholders. The three Cs are there to keep the ecosystem in balance in order to increase the entire enterprise's potential for success.

Key Pieces:

- Internal collaboration provides greater cooperation, improved communication and strengthens relationships with the workforce and organizational functions.

- The successful use of the trinity of strategies, tactics, and execution vigilance by the workforce increases the probability for success.

- Strategic thinking works best when there is a diverse cross-section of expertise and skill sets from within the organization.

- Tactical planning is enhanced by the participation of a diverse group of skilled and experienced personnel who generate effective results.

- Execution initiatives are those operating fronts which have the charter to complete tasks outlined by the tactical approach, while acting as an execution road map.

- The three Cs of effective operations are communication, cooperation and commitment.

- The recognition of the three Cs and the use of self-directed, cross-functional teams are safeguards for keeping the organizational ecosystem in balance.

SECTION SIX

The Process of Evolving

THE PROCESS OF EVOLVING

"**W**hy are we changing?" asks the employee. "We are changing, because we are not satisfied with where we are, what we are doing, how we are doing it and the results we are getting," replies a company leader.

Depending on who in the company gives the above response, this statement could be the first move required to begin your journey toward change. The level of change required for an existing organization's becoming a Collaborative Enterprise can only materialize through an evolutionary process. Realizing there is a need for change is the necessary first step in the evolutionary process, but knowing that a change must be made is no guarantee that the change will occur.

The common factor between whether to deploy an evolutionary or revolutionary process is the knowledge that waves of change are coming and they must be addressed. The key differences between an evolutionary and a revolutionary change process are the intensity and duration. I believe that the only type of company that could possibly join the ranks of a Collaborative Enterprise through *revolutionary* means is a very small company with a change in leadership totally committed to the conversion to a Collaborative Enterprise culture.

More established organizations, large or small, cannot venture into a revolutionary change without materially impacting the overall performance of the corporation. Regardless of the commitment on the part of the management team, the owners and Board of Directors would not be willing to take the hit to the bottom line and stock price, if publicly traded, that would occur from the drastic changes required to the culture of the organization.

If the leadership knows they want to change to a CE environment and have read the previous chapters, they now know the attributes needed to be deployed. The question then becomes: How do they begin the evolutionary process? They need to eat the elephant with one small bite at a time, and my advice would be, "Know what you do best, and continue to improve it."

CEs focus on providing, in the most effective and efficient manner, their products and services to their customers. They are as committed to *how* they produce as much as they are to *what* they produce.

Effectiveness and efficiency require the long-term commitment to a change in culture. A sustainable, lasting change in culture is advised for the same reason airline pilots fly with an automatic pilot. It would be too exhausting for a pilot to fly a long distance manually. A demand and control leadership style is too exhausting for the management team to expect over the long term in order to increase effectiveness and efficiency. I surmise that is the reason for the high degree of turnover in executives, after five to seven years of service.

The evolutionary change process will be effective in moving the culture forward in a positive direction when the organization begins with a commitment to the new delegate and coach style of management and to "continuous improvement." If the organization's products or services are reasonably successful in the market, then the enterprise knows it has a stepping-stone from which to work. Their motto could be, "Let's do what we do, only do it better, each and every day."

Staying focused on the goals and objectives is important, because there will be challenges, doubts, fears, insecurities, and failures. These conditions are a part of the change process. Those committed to the change have the challenge to retain their commitment and stay focused on the overall, long-term goal of becoming a dominating participant in their market or industry.

Concentrating on the goal over a long period of time is extremely difficult. It takes a special combination of owners, directors and top executives to sustain the energy and commitment until the culture begins to transform and increased positive results begin to materialize. Once the improvement *momentum* is visible, the task of moving forward becomes easier. I call that the "momentum flywheel effect." It all starts with "one step at a time."

Each step along the evolutionary path leads to an overall goal of maintaining a sustainable organization. Any organization can show high profits, outstanding capital valuations and worldwide-recognized brands, but are they going to be sustainable? It's a marathon, not a sprint. We have heard that many times and it is often true.

Leadership and technologies come and go, but cultures are slow to change. Maintained properly, cultures are the automatic pilot for the enterprise.

The Collaborative Enterprise knows that the transformed culture can produce many positive side-effects beyond market dominance and bottom-line results. There is also, a fully-engaged workforce and stakeholders; a pool of highly-motivated, skilled executives and managers, who are ready to take on greater responsibilities; and a positive operating environment which takes great pride in doing things better each day.

A close friend reminded me of one of his favorite sayings: "*Competitors can steal your ideas, products, employees, etc.; but, they can never steal your culture and that is one of the best competitive advantages you can have.*" The Collaborative Enterprise is not looking for publicity, but once acknowledged for its results, it is held in reverence by the rest of the industry and beyond.

In your quest for deciding whether or not you or your corporation or organization is a candidate for becoming a Collaborative Enterprise or participating in one, I want you to think of three words; *Knowledge, Belief, and Doing.*

Knowledge is about what a Collaborative Enterprise is, how it works, and why it does what it does. The potential rewards of its actions are now in your hands. You now know what it takes to be a Collaborative Enterprise.

Belief is about a level of commitment you now have to your newly-found knowledge and understanding of the Collaborative Enterprise. It is about how deeply you believe in what you now know.

Doing deals with just that: doing — by moving forward with a commitment, a vision and a plan. You are taking that first step and hopefully knowing you are not going to stop. Your first step does not need to be a commitment to an entire Collaborative Enterprise renovation project. A first step may be a new focus on "continuous improvement". It may be improving your communications with your stakeholders and internal departments. That first step may be to introduce the concept of delegation and coaching to your leadership. Your first step may be to put into practice some of the suggestions you have learned from this book just within your own area of control. By doing, you are separating yourself from the planners, strategists, and talkers; and, that makes you, "forever better."

If you should decide to pursue the challenge, I wish you well in your decision to join the ever-growing population of Collaborative Enterprises that are becoming dominant in their markets and their industries — each and every day.

12 Steps for Becoming a More Effective Businessperson

1. Do your work before you play.

2. Always do more than others expect of you.

3. Never stop trying to become better at something.

4. Be willing to do the things you don't like to do in order to achieve what you want.

5. Be willing to accept failure and disappointment as a part of learning.

6. Recognize that there is no easy or quick way to gain experience.

7. Take time to appreciate the things you usually take for granted.

8. Be honest in everything you do and honor your word when you make a promise to do something, *even* if it becomes inconvenient.

9. Respect the feelings and property of others.

10. Have a desire to and take action to help others.

11. Never stop learning.

12. Recognize that situations in life are never as bad or as good as they may seem and that you are never alone.

ABOUT THE AUTHOR

Robert Nitschke is currently founder and managing partner of Arago Partners LLC, an independent consulting firm providing operations and performance renovation leadership services to clients, nationally and internationally. *"Don't confuse efforts with results"*. Robert's decades of relentless drive to achieve remarkable results by introducing collaboration and a focus on continuous improvement have gained him the respect of his clients, associates and peers. His extraordinary work ethic and desire to be an organizational problem solver continues to provide him with the tenacity and drive to serve where problem issues or initiatives dwell.

Robert has more than three decades of business experience, spanning a wide range of skills, experiences and industries. He has held executive and managerial positions in operations and information technology within several Fortune 500 companies and has invested over ten years in support of turnaround and early stage entrepreneurial ventures. Robert's results driven spirit has produced successes in telecommunication, manufacturing, ecommerce, International project finance, cruise-tour and service enterprises.

Robert believes in helping others. He serves non-profit organizations that reach out to abused children, providing medical and mobility equipment for low income people stricken with Multiple Sclerosis and teaching children the benefits of staying in school.

Robert is a continual learner. He is a graduate of the University of Washington, the highly recognized Tepper School of Business at Carnegie Mellon University, and holds Certifications in Lean Operations and Project Management. He is proud to have served the United States Army Security Agency and participated in the Viet Nam Campaign. He teaches at local colleges, publishes business articles for local and web-based distribution and sits on the Boards of Advisors for local companies.

To know more about Robert L. Nitschke, visit:
www.creatingacollaborativeenterprise.com
http://www.linkedin.com/in/rnitschke

To know more about Arago Partners LLC, visit:
www.aragopartnersllc.com
www.aragopartnersllc.com/bulletin
www.twitter.com/aragopartners